What Leaders Are Saying

"Through these pages, Aaron Früh will escort you down an ancient pathway and show you how to break the cycle of transgenerational sin—often the fruit of verbal abuse. Healing the tongue, he says, can mend and refresh the human heart, the home and the family. I believe you will be inspired and challenged by this man's candor and honesty, as well as his passion about learning how, why and when to speak these blessings."

from the foreword by **Bill McCartney**,
founder/chairman, The Road to Jerusalem

"If you want to grasp the weeds of rejection and pull them up by the roots, read this book. The teaching concerning generational curses has developed over the last several years. Aaron Früh effectively enlarges the scope of this principle with his belief that many generational wounds are caused by verbal abuse. If you are dealing with inner bruises caused by a cursing tongue, I highly recommend this book. Pastor Aaron's fresh approach, mixed with many of his own life stories, makes this book a fascinating journey toward healing."

Michelle McKinney Hammond, author,
Why Do I Say "Yes" When I Need to Say "No"?

"I smile from deep within when I think of Aaron Früh's pilgrimage, of his discovery of his Jewishness and the enormous revelation that the Lord is giving him as a result of putting all this together. Enter the pilgrimage with this man of God. Listen to the passion of his heart and begin your own pilgrimage (if you have not yet done so) that brings all of us into the richness that comes from our parent family of faith, the family of Abraham, Isaac and Israel."

Don Finto, pastor emeritus, Belmont Church; founder/director, The Caleb Company

"Aaron Früh adds an important link in the growing understanding and application of the Jewish roots of Christianity. The power of blessing—the verbal reinforcement of the requirements and blessings of the covenant—becomes a life-changing force for helping to build strong families and godly lives. This book will show you one of life's hidden keys—small actions, done in faith and obedience, that can make a great difference in your life and the lives of those you love. I strongly encourage you to read and apply the powerful lessons in this book!"

Robert Stearns, founder and executive director, Eagles' Wings

THE
FORGOTTEN
BLESSING

Ancient Words That Heal Generational Wounds

AARON FRÜH

Chosen
Grand Rapids, Michigan

Published by Chosen Books
a division of Baker Publishing Group
P.O. Box 6287, Grand Rapids, MI 49516-6287
www.chosenbooks.com

Printed in the United States of America

Library of Congress Cataloging-in-Publication Data
Früh, Aaron, 1958–
    The forgotten blessing : ancient words that heal generational wounds / Aaron Früh.
        p.   cm.
    Includes bibliographical references.
    ISBN 10: 0-8007-9402-8 (pbk.)
    ISBN 978-0-8007-9402-6 (pbk.)
    1. Blessing and cursing. 2. Christian life. I. Title.
BV4509.5.F78 2006
248.8'45—dc22   2005023571

For Rose Krupnick,
my Jewish grandmother,
who taught me about the forgotten blessing

Contents

Foreword

The power of verbal blessing has been hidden to Gentiles for generations. Yet God ordained this pathway, and to the Jewish people it remains a cherished part of everyday life. It is a pathway that will lead to healing and restoration.

The Church has all but forgotten this ancient practice, and as a result, we are missing opportunities to use this potent tool to counter the effects of iniquity in our world, our communities and even our homes.

"I am convinced," says Pastor Aaron Früh, "that throughout redemptive history God has ordained the verbal blessing to be the fountainhead to counter the curse of sin."

Our words matter. They can bring life, or they can bring destruction. It is no secret that I believe if you really want to know about a man, and if you want to know what kind of character he has, you need only look at the countenance of his wife. Everything he has invested, or withheld, can be found there. Including his words.

Our words can build up, or they can destroy. We have all seen the irreparable damage caused by evil words. And we have marveled at the power of encouraging and positive words—and the humility often required to use them. God can use our words to heal marriages and family relationships.

Through these pages, Aaron Früh will escort you down this ancient pathway and show you how to break the cycle of trans-generational sin—often the fruit of verbal abuse. Healing the tongue, he says, can mend and refresh the human heart, the home and the family.

I believe you will be inspired and challenged by this man's candor and honesty, as well as his passion about learning how, why and when to speak these blessings.

Bill McCartney
Founder/chairman, The Road to Jerusalem

The Forgotten Blessing

Clearing Your Lost Pathway

So he blessed them that day, saying, "By you Israel will bless, saying, 'May God make you as Ephraim and as Manasseh!'"

Genesis 48:20

I recently ventured into my front yard to trim back the vastly overgrown hedges. It was a hot, muggy Gulf Coast day in the middle of August. If you have never lived in the Deep South, let me assure you that this is not considered an enjoyable summer activity. But nothing was going to stop me on this day—not even 100-degree heat with 100 percent humidity! I was on a Lewis and Clark expedition. They were commissioned by the government to find a passageway to the Pacific; I was commissioned by my wife to find a passageway through the overgrown brush to our backyard.

Ever since we had purchased the house several months earlier, I had wondered why the original builders had not put in a sidewalk or path of some kind to link the front yard with the back. I talked to a carpenter about it, and he agreed with me. Since the house sits on a sloping hillside, he told me that if I would clear away the overgrown brush and trim back the native azalea bushes, he would build a wooden stairway to connect the two yards.

I woke early that Saturday morning in order to get a jump on the project before the heat index hit its peak. By eight o'clock I was drenched with sweat. If Lewis and Clark had been trying to find a passage to the Gulf of Mexico instead of a path to the Pacific, I am pretty sure they would have died of heat exhaustion somewhere in the vicinity of my front yard.

By eleven o'clock great piles of branches, thorns and thistles had accumulated, but still no sight of the backyard. Then at two o'clock, my tree trimmer made a loud scraping sound. Thinking I had bumped into a rock or a concrete marker of some kind, I pulled back more branches to investigate further. What I saw amazed me. There before me stood a brick retaining wall!

I began to cut frantically along the edges of the wall, and within an hour I uncovered an architecturally designed retaining wall that bordered the entire side yard of the house. By cutting back even more brush, I discovered my "passageway to the Pacific"! For lying hidden under that vegetative rubble was a brick stairway that led down into the backyard.

This handsome, long-forgotten brickwork has once again become what it was designed to be—a useful pathway that leads from one landscape to the next.

Seeking an Ancient Pathway

Jeremiah the prophet talks about the importance of not forgetting the ancient pathways of truth: "Thus says the LORD: 'Stand in the ways and see, and ask for the old paths, where the good way is, and walk in it; then you will find rest for your souls'" (Jeremiah 6:16). In this book we will uncover one of these "old paths"—a "good way" that has become overgrown with thistles and thorns from years of neglect.

Please understand that our journey will not be easy. Finding and clearing ancient passageways is hard work. This was true even in "ancient" times! For centuries—millennia—people have struggled with finding their way, usually with the question of *Why?* on their lips. Why is it so hard to walk in paths that should be receptive to our footsteps? Why does it seem to take forever to realize a promise? Listen to the question of the matriarch Rebecca when she was carrying the twins Jacob and Esau: "The children struggled together within her; and she said, 'If all is well, why am I like this?'" (Genesis 25:22).

Have you ever asked this question? "Lord, if all is well, why am I like this? If all is well, why do I still feel the pain of rejection? Why do I feel shame, insecurity and isolation? If all is well, why do I feel this gnawing emptiness and loneliness? If all is well, why am I like this?"

Like many others, you probably came to faith with the expectation that you soon would be climbing newfound paths with hind's feet in high places. But whenever you came close to finding the passageway to your purpose and happiness, something frustrated your attempt; you never seemed to be able to move forward. As time passed, more thorns and bushes blocked your progress. Now it seems as if the passageway to God's good promises for your life is completely overgrown and, if not forgotten, at least unattainable. And yet you know that deeper fulfillment is possible.

Let me ask you a question. Have you ever compared yourself unfavorably with others? Have you ever looked at another person—someone with wholeness, well-being, stability, graciousness—and wondered, *If all is well, why am I not like him or her? Why do I never feel that I am "good enough"? Why do I never measure up?*

Have these thoughts entered your mind, even fleetingly? If so, this is a fairly certain indication that your pathway to promise has been blocked to some extent by the thorns and briars of abusive words—to be more specific, words that have acted like curses in your life. I can say without hesitation that every person who has been verbally belittled, shamed or abused carries inside a feeling of being "different." It is also true that most of the whole and complete people we compare ourselves to had parents or caregivers who consistently spoke words of blessing into their lives.

I believe that the level of emotional stability that we enjoy in adulthood is directly linked to the amount of verbal blessing we received in childhood. I also believe that the level of emotional instability that we experience is directly linked to the kinds of abusive verbal curses we endured in childhood.

Can an ancient pathway of truth lead us to wholeness? If so, is it possible to discover it and tear away the thorns and weeds and prickly bushes that block our way? The answer on both counts is yes. Together we will discover the life-changing ancient pathway of the spoken blessing. We will learn what it is, how it works and the further consequences in our lives of its neglect.

The Start of Our Journey

In chapter 5 of our study together I will share with you the personal odyssey that led me to discover this ancient path. Let me tell you up front, however, that I am of Jewish descent. I uncovered the ancient path of spoken blessing several years ago while visiting my family in Tel Aviv, Israel. One thing became clear as I observed the lifestyle of Jewish people living in the Holy Land: They consistently speak words of blessing and affirmation to one another.

The words they speak today are the same words they have spoken for thousands of years. God provided these ancient and powerful blessings and meant for all Israel, including the Church, to use them—along with many other appropriate words of blessing. Over the centuries, however, as many traditions were rejected or filtered out of practical application, the Church lost sight of this important action.

Orthodox Jewish families, however, have not. If you venture into the home of any Orthodox Jewish family anywhere in the world during a Friday evening Shabbat celebration, you will hear several blessings spoken by the parents.

The father begins. After the meal is over, he calls his sons to his side and lays his hands upon their heads. Then he proclaims a blessing: "May you be like Ephraim and Manasseh."

Ephraim and Manasseh? What is that all about? We will return to this blessing throughout our journey, but let me give you a brief background.

Two sons were born to Joseph while he was in Egypt. The first son he named *Manasseh*, which means "making forgetful." Joseph said, "For God has made me forget all my toil and all my father's house" (Genesis 41:51).

The second son he named *Ephraim*, which means "fruitfulness." In choosing this name Joseph said, "For God has caused me to be fruitful in the land of my affliction" (Genesis 41:52).

Joseph had been rejected by his father and his brothers because of his prophetic dreams. In fact, the Bible says that his brothers could not speak a kind word to him (see Genesis 37:4). They sold him into slavery, and he spent the next twenty years as a slave and prisoner. Joseph gave his sons very significant names! He desired to forget all the pain and hatred he endured in his father's house, place it in his past and bear fruit in his future.

Later, when Joseph was restored to his father and his brothers, he brought the two boys to his father, Jacob, to bless, and here is the blessing pronounced by Jacob: "So he blessed them that day, saying, 'By you Israel will bless, saying, "May God make you as Ephraim and as Manasseh!"'" (Genesis 48:20).

Jacob was saying, "All of Israel will bless her children with this blessing: May God cause you to forget the pain of your past and make you fruitful and prosperous in your future!" Each father who continues this practice today is speaking by faith that his children will forget the pain of their past and bear fruit in their future. (Is it any wonder that Jewish people are the most fruitful people in the world?)

The mothers, in turn, gather their daughters to them and lay their hands upon their heads as they proclaim this blessing from Ruth 4:11:

> The LORD make the woman who is coming to your house like Rachel and Leah, the two who built the house of Israel; and may you prosper in Ephrathah and be famous in Bethlehem.

After the children have been blessed, the husband will then bless his wife with a reading from Proverbs 31:

> Who can find a virtuous wife? For her worth is far above rubies. The heart of her husband safely trusts her; so he will have no lack of gain. She does him good and not evil all the days of her life. . . . Her husband is known in the gates, when he sits among the elders of the land. . . . Her

children rise up and call her blessed; her husband also, and he praises her: "Many daughters have done well, but you excel them all." Charm is deceitful and beauty is passing, but a woman who fears the LORD, she shall be praised. Give her of the fruit of her hands, and let her own works praise her in the gates.

Proverbs 31:10–12, 23, 28–31

When the husband has finished blessing his wife, she then blesses him with the words of Psalm 128:

Your wife shall be like a fruitful vine in the very heart of your house, your children like olive plants all around your table. Behold, thus shall the man be blessed who fears the LORD. The LORD bless you out of Zion, and may you see the good of Jerusalem all the days of your life. Yes, may you see your children's children.

Psalm 128:3–6

The closest we come in Christian circles to walking the ancient path of verbal blessing is in some of the more traditional churches, where at the close of the services the priests or pastors still pray the Aaronic blessing over their congregations:

And the LORD spoke to Moses, saying: "Speak to Aaron and his sons, saying, 'This is the way you shall bless the children of Israel. Say to them: "The LORD bless you and keep you; the LORD make His face shine upon you, and be gracious to you; the LORD lift up His countenance upon you, and give you peace."' So they shall put My name on the children of Israel, and I will bless them."

Numbers 6:22–27

The Hebrew word for blessing is *barak*. It means "to praise, confer a blessing and to bend the knee." Often the recipient of blessing would kneel down when the blessing

17

was pronounced over him by another. The Greek word for blessing is *eulogeo*. When broken down, the meaning of the word is clear: *eu* means "good" and *logos* means "word." Thus, in Greek the word *blessing* means "to speak a good word" concerning someone or something.

When God called Abraham, He said: "I will make you a great nation; I will bless you and make your name great; and you shall be a blessing. I will bless those who bless you, and I will curse him who curses you; and in you all the families of the earth shall be blessed" (Genesis 12:2–3).

Remember that the word *blessing* means to "speak well" of another. So God was actually saying to Abraham: "Whoever confers verbal blessing upon you, I will confer verbal blessing upon him. Whoever speaks well of you, I will speak well of him."

Later God extended this principle to all of Abraham's children, whether descended from him physically or spiritually. After providing the ram in the thicket for Abraham to sacrifice in substitution for his son Isaac, God said:

> [In] blessing I will bless you, and [in] multiplying I will multiply your descendants as the stars of the heaven and as the sand which is on the seashore; and your descendants shall possess the gate of their enemies.
>
> Genesis 22:17

This verse makes it clear: As we bless others, so in turn God blesses us, and in addition, we are rewarded with the gates of our enemies. In my blessing of others—even those who have cursed me— is found my own blessing!

Could it be, then, that giving and receiving verbal blessing is God's way for His people to counteract hell's councils and reverse the flow of iniquity from generation to generation? Could it also be God's way of bringing wholeness, completion and healing to those who never received a spoken blessing from those who should have blessed them?

I believe so. *I am convinced that throughout redemptive history God has ordained that the verbal blessing be the key passageway that counters the effects of the curse of sin caused by the Fall.*

The focus of our study will be the one blessing that I call the "forgotten blessing," those words the patriarch Jacob spoke over his grandsons: "So he blessed them that day, saying, 'By you Israel will bless, saying, "May God make you as Ephraim and as Manasseh!"'" This is the pattern for the descendants of Abraham; it is the foundation for all of Israel's blessing.

It is wonderful to consider that every member of the Body of Christ who is not already of Jewish heritage is supernaturally grafted into the family of Abraham, Isaac and Jacob, so this blessing is meant for us as well! This is the way that Israel—that you and I—will bless and be blessed. It is the way that generations of verbal cursing will be eradicated. It is the way that we will find healing and restoration for ourselves and the generations to come.

Our lives will never be the same.

A Thing of the Past?

Once I started down this forgotten pathway by studying the power of verbal blessing, I was amazed that we could have forgotten a discipline that was so prevalent in Christ's life and ministry.

When Jesus was presented to the Lord as an infant at the Temple in Jerusalem, a man named Simeon took Jesus up in his arms, blessed God and said this:

"Lord, now You are letting Your servant depart in peace, according to Your word; for my eyes have seen Your salvation which You have prepared before the face of all peoples, a light to bring revelation to the Gentiles, and the glory of Your people Israel." And Joseph and His mother marveled at those things which were spoken of Him. Then Simeon blessed them, and said to Mary His mother, "Behold, this Child is destined for the fall and rising of many in Israel."

Luke 2:29–34

The gospel of Mark tells us that a group of parents brought their children to Jesus so He could lay His hands on them and confer a blessing upon their young lives. Mark records:

Then they brought little children to Him, that He might touch them; but the disciples rebuked those who brought them. But when Jesus saw it, He was greatly displeased and said to them, "Let the little children come to Me, and do not forbid them; for of such is the kingdom of God. Assuredly, I say to you, whoever does not receive the kingdom of God as a little child will by no means enter it." And He took them up in His arms, laid His hands on them, and blessed them.

Mark 10:13–16

When Jesus took them up into His arms and blessed them, what did He say? Did He proclaim the forgotten blessing and declare that they would be like Ephraim and Manasseh? It is quite possible.

Jesus was blessed verbally at birth. He blessed others verbally during His ministry, and after His death and resurrection we see this beautiful example of blessing at His ascension:

And He led them out as far as Bethany, and He lifted up His hands and blessed them. Now it came to pass, while He blessed them, that He was parted from them and carried up into heaven.

Luke 24:50–51

Picture it: As Jesus ascended into the clouds of heaven, His hands were outstretched toward His disciples and He spoke words of blessing over them.

Yet today many in the Church consider Jesus' example a thing of the past. When I first began to understand the power of verbal blessing, I asked my nine-year-old daughter, Hannah, to sit beside me on the couch so that I could speak a blessing over her. She looked up at me with a startled look and exclaimed: "But Daddy, I didn't sneeze!" When you stop and think about it, the only time Christians use the word *bless* is when someone sneezes ("Bless you!") or when we pray for a meal ("Bless this food to our bodies").

Verbal cursing has taken much from you, and since the Church has largely forgotten the ancient pathway of verbal blessing, you have not known about a major instrument of warfare to counter it. The effects of the curse of iniquity are many; it is time to walk on a new pathway.

As we tear away the thorns and brush that have hidden the forgotten blessing, you will learn how to restore what has been lost in your life. You will see how words from generations past have affected you for good or evil—and how those words will affect future generations.

Basically, you will learn more about yourself—your true name, the journey that is your own personal story, the purpose for which God created you and even the promise that He has given you.

It is my premise that much of the iniquity that is being passed from generation to generation is a result of verbal abuse. And if that is the case, *if it was through the tongue that we were cursed, then I believe it is through the tongue that healing and blessing will come.* If we can heal the tongue, we can heal and restore the human heart, the home and the family, and ultimately generations to come. Will you take a walk with me down this ancient pathway? There are some things I would like to show you—things that I have discovered in my own odyssey and that I think will restore hope and healing to you as they have to me.

 2

Bless Me, Too!

Why You Believe Negative Things about Yourself

When Esau heard the words of his father, he cried with
an exceedingly great and bitter cry, and said to his father,
"Bless me—me also, O my father!"

Genesis 27:34

The door closed behind me with a thud of finality. It was
another cold, gray January day in the city of Chicago, and
I had been called to the North Side Juvenile Detention
Center by a worried mother. She had attended our Sunday
morning service just the day before and had given her
life to Jesus. She was a Jewish woman in her middle
fifties who still bore the numbers on her forearm from
the Nazi death camp Auschwitz, having been taken there
from Warsaw, Poland, as a young girl. She also bore the
emotional scars of a Holocaust survivor.

Now once again she faced barbed wire and prison doors—this time from the outside. She had asked that her thirteen-year-old daughter, Lea, be incarcerated after her third runaway attempt. The mother told me that Lea's young heart was incapable of forming any kind of emotional bond or loving relationship because of the years of rejection and physical abuse she had suffered from her now-absent Gentile father.

As I followed the female security guard through long corridors of locked doors, I wondered what I would face when I met Lea for the first time. Would she be hard and cold? Would I be an unwelcome intruder to her now-antiseptic world of painted-white concrete walls, gray blankets and the smell of industrial disinfectant? Would she give me eye contact, or would she regard me as just another likely candidate for the long list of men who had taken advantage of her?

We rounded the corner to the visitation room, and time stood still for a moment. Lea sat alone in the corner of the empty room. Her back was toward the door; she faced the wall of windows, watching the quiet parking lot and the lightly falling snow. Her hair was bleached blonde—a trademark of the hard-driving punk rock of the 1980s in which we lived. I approached cautiously. With every step I asked the Lord for words to speak to this despairing young girl. When I reached the corner of the visitation room, I spoke her name: "Lea." What happened next will be forever recorded in my memory.

When I called Lea's name she was not startled. She had no feeling left for fear. Her head turned gradually toward me, as if the gears of a machine were slowly turning. What I saw when her face—shrouded by her long, dead-white hair—came into view will forever haunt me. To my surprise, I did not see a cold, hardened heart. Instead I found myself looking into sunken, haunted eyes that were pleading: *What about me? Won't someone—god or devil—care about me, too? Can't someone, someone on earth, someone in heaven or in hell, bless me, too?*

What I learned from this encounter with two survivors of two different kinds of holocausts is that every person who lacks a father's blessing is something like Lea. If someone could sit in the empty visitation rooms of our hearts, and we slowly, mechanically turned our faces toward that one, he would see the same empty eyes. He would find the same desperate souls, hoping for some visitor—any visitor—who will carry a word of blessing! There are multitudes in our generation, and multitudes upon multitudes behind, crying out, "Won't someone—anyone—bless me, too?"

Desperate Measures

We saw in our first chapter how Jacob blessed his two grandsons and proclaimed that through those two boys the nation of Israel would forever bless their children by saying: "May you be like Ephraim and Manasseh." Jacob, of all people, knew the significance and power of receiving a verbal blessing.

You see, Jacob had a twin brother named Esau. You talk about sibling rivalry, they had it! In those days the father's best blessing always went to the oldest son, and Jacob missed being eligible for this blessing by only a few seconds—after losing a physical struggle with Esau while they were still in their mother's womb. It was this ongoing struggle even before their birth that brought out the cry of the matriarch Rebekah that we mentioned in the last chapter: "If all is well, why am I like this?"

Let's look at how this story unfolds:

Now Isaac pleaded with the Lord for his wife, because she was barren; and the Lord granted his plea, and Rebekah his wife conceived. But the children struggled together within her; and she said, "If all is well, why am I like this?" So she went to inquire of the LORD. And the LORD said to her: "Two nations are in your womb, two peoples shall be separated from your body; one people shall be stronger than the other, and the older shall serve the younger." So when her days were fulfilled for her to give birth, indeed there were twins in her womb. And the first came out red. He was like a hairy garment all over; so they called his name Esau. Afterward his brother came out, and his hand took hold of Esau's heel; so his name was called Jacob. Isaac was sixty years old when she bore them.

So the boys grew. And Esau was a skillful hunter, a man of the field; but Jacob was a mild man, dwelling in tents. And Isaac loved Esau because he ate of his game, but Rebekah loved Jacob.

Genesis 25:21–28

Jacob grew up desperate for his father's attention and blessing, but he was disqualified by his birth order and by his father's favoritism. (The patriarchal families were indeed less than perfect!) Esau would legitimately receive from his father "a double portion of all that he has, for he is the beginning of his strength; the right of the firstborn is his" (Deuteronomy 21:17). But—perhaps due to Isaac's favoritism—jealousy for his father's attention and the blessing of the birthright began to close around Jacob's spirit like the jaws of a trap. Soon Jacob began working to fulfill the meaning of his name, "supplanter," in a way that has permanently given that name a second meaning: "deceiver."

Now Jacob cooked a stew; and Esau came in from the field, and he was weary. And Esau said to Jacob, "Please feed me with that same red stew, for I am weary." Therefore his name was called Edom [red]. But Jacob said, "Sell me your birthright as of this day." And Esau said, "Look, I am about to die; so what is this birthright to me?" Then Jacob said, "Swear to me as of this day." So he swore to him, and sold his birthright to Jacob. And Jacob gave Esau bread and stew of lentils; then he ate and drank, arose, and went his way. Thus Esau despised his birthright.

Genesis 25:29–34

A man could sell his birthright to his brother, according to the custom of the day, so now the only thing Jacob lacked was his father's verbal blessing. To receive that he would have to deceive his father into believing he was Esau. When his brother was out in the field hunting game, Jacob dressed in animal skins to mimic his hairy brother and took savory food and bread to his father, who was nearly blind.

Jacob said to his father, "I am Esau your firstborn; I have done just as you told me; please arise, sit and eat of my game, that your soul may bless me." . . . And [Jacob] came near and kissed him; and he smelled the smell of his clothing, and blessed him and said: "Surely, the smell of my son is like the smell of a field which the LORD has blessed. Therefore may God give you of the dew of heaven, of the fatness of the earth, and plenty of grain and wine. Let peoples serve you, and nations bow down to you. Be master over your brethren, and let your mother's sons bow down to you. Cursed be everyone who curses you, and blessed be those who bless you!"

Genesis 27:19, 27–29

Soon after Jacob received the blessing, in came his brother Esau with his own pot of stew and he said:

"Let my father arise and eat of his son's game, that your soul may bless me." And his father Isaac said to him,

"Who are you?" So he said, "I am your son, your first-born, Esau." Then Isaac trembled exceedingly, and said, "Who? Where is the one who hunted game and brought it to me? I ate all of it before you came, and I have blessed him—and indeed he shall be blessed." When Esau heard the words of his father, he cried with an exceedingly great and bitter cry, and said to his father, "Bless me—me also, O my father!"

Genesis 27:31–34

One thing is clear from this story: People are desperate for verbal blessing, will go to any lengths to receive it and are crushed when they lose it. The cry of every person's heart in our generation—young or old—is: "Bless me—me, too!"

The Pain of Feeling "Defective"

The unfathomable tragedy in Lea's story is that it is not unique. There are millions of Leas who have been crippled by receiving verbal abuse from a parent or care-giver. This cursing takes two forms: One is the destruction of verbal assault. When a person hears words such as "you are worthless," it is only a matter of time before she begins to believe them. The other is the devastating lack of speech altogether, which also carries deadly consequences for one's identity and destiny. When a person never receives affirmation, never hears reassuring or positive words like "I love you" or "I'm proud of you" or even words of simple encouragement like "You can do it," his inner confidence slips away in the silence, and the void fills with feelings of worthlessness.

You see, verbal blessing and affirmation are emotional building blocks vital for personal growth and development. Listen to the following wisdom from the book of Proverbs:

A man has joy by the answer of his mouth, and a word spoken in due season, how good it is!

> Proverbs 15:23

A word fitly spoken is like apples of gold in settings of silver.

> Proverbs 25:11

Anxiety in the heart of man causes depression, but a good word makes it glad.

> Proverbs 12:25

Andrew Vachss, an attorney who has committed his life to protecting children from abuse, writes this about emotional abuse:

Emotional abuse threatens to become a national illness. The emotional abuse of children can lead, in adulthood, to addiction, rage, a severely damaged sense of self and an inability to truly bond with others. Of all the forms of child abuse, emotional abuse may be the cruelest and longest lasting of all. Emotional abuse is the systematic diminishment of another. It is designed to reduce a child's self-concept to the point where the victim considers himself unworthy—unworthy of respect, unworthy of friendship, unworthy of the natural birthright of all children: love and protection.

Emotional abuse can be as deliberate as a gunshot: "You're fat. You're stupid. You're ugly."

Emotional abuse can be active: "You'll never be the success your brother was. I'm ashamed you're my son." . . .

Emotional abuse conditions the child to expect abuse in later life. Emotional abuse is a time bomb, but its effects are rarely visible, because the emotionally abused tend to implode, turning the anger against themselves. "[1]

29

The gist of what happened to Lea was that her identity was defiled. Her father's silent rejection, punctuated by destructive tirades, had left her drinking from the wellspring of shame. Once our identity is cursed, shame becomes the basis of our existence, the filter through which every thought and emotion is processed. Our view of others and our concept of the future is radically altered and contorted by this filter of shame.

Saying "I made a mistake" is healthy and comes from well-balanced introspection. But shame takes one beyond "I made a mistake" to the abyss of "I am a mistake." Shame is a feeling of being defective, of being infected and quarantined with a rare disease that has no cure.

A person who lives in shame ultimately concludes that she is a human Humpty Dumpty that all the king's horses and all the king's men cannot put back together again. A person whose identity has been cursed will live either under the banner of extreme worthlessness or under the banner of artificial independence and self-sufficiency.

As you read these words, do you have a sense of identification? Do you think that this might apply to you? See if you consistently experience any of these emotions and behaviors:

Worthlessness; Anger when circumstances are out of control; Fear of emotion; Fear of experiencing feelings; Fear of losing control; Difficulty saying "NO"; Fear of trying new things; Fear of failure or failing; Dependence, codependence; Walking in reluctant responsibility; Walking in false responsibility; Frequent depression; compulsive sin or addiction; Need to succeed in order to be accepted; Procrastination; Independence and self-sufficiency; Isolation—difficulty making close friends; Avoidance of getting into a position of need or dependence; Difficulty asking a favor or for help; A better giver than receiver; Fear of discomfort being in a small group without being the leader; Discomfort being in a small group; Feeling of

30

being tolerated rather than chosen; Having been a recipient, feeling a need to repay; Restlessness; Compulsion—drawn to schemes to make money.[2]

Dear one, if you identify with any of these descriptions, your experiences may be in some measure like Lea's. Take heart and be encouraged, because we will discover in the coming chapters that you do not have to maneuver circumstances like Jacob in order to receive blessing. In fact, you have always been seated at the head of the table—only you did not know it! In our next chapter we are going to see how verbal blessing works to restore true identity to the human heart, counteracting the defilement of shame.

 3

What Is Your Name?

Birthing Your True Identity

So He said to him, "What is your name?" He said, "Jacob."

Genesis 32:27

You and I went through a lot just to enter this world. Our very first nine months were spent in an intense crash course on human development! At least we were living in the protective surroundings of our mothers' wombs—until, without being given a choice, we were dropped into a birth canal and squeezed beyond recognition. With a shock, like waking up to the sound of thunder, we appeared in the cold hands of a birth doctor who was intent on slapping our posteriors and directing every bright light in the room toward ground zero where we landed.

But then something wonderful and beyond understanding happened to us—we were wrapped carefully in swaddling clothes, and placed in our mothers' arms. Our heart rates came under control as we were calmed by our mothers' beating hearts. But the best was yet to come, because psychologists tell us that a newborn is not really quite at peace until she looks up into the shining face of her mother. The moment when a baby sees her mother's face—and the acceptance, love and tenderness expressed there—is the moment when the newborn is completely calmed, now safe from fear in her mother's arms. I find it interesting that psychologists also say that the soothing face of the mother is the umbilical cord to a child's soul.

What if, by a series of unfortunate events, that umbilical cord of unconditional love and acceptance were severed by a parent or a caregiver? Or what if it never connected in the first place because those mothers were unhappy about or embittered by the arrival of a child and were unable to reach out emotionally? What would happen to our souls—our human emotions? In an article entitled "Bonding and Attachment in Maltreated Children," Bruce Perry, Duane Runyan and Carrie Sturges state:

> Human relationships take many forms but the most intense, most pleasurable and most painful are those relationships with family, friends and loved ones. Within this inner circle of intimate relationships, we are bonded to each other with "emotional glue"—bonded with love.[3]

These authors make it clear that developing intimate relationships later in life is difficult if a person was not nurtured and loved at a young age:

> They feel no "pull" to form intimate relationships, find little pleasure in being with or close to others. They have few, if any friends and more distant, less emotional glue

with family. In extreme cases an individual may have no intact emotional bond to any other person. They are self-absorbed and aloof. Experiences during this early vulnerable period of life are critical to shaping the capacity to form intimate and emotionally healthy relationships. Empathy, caring, sharing, and capacity to love and a host of other characteristics of a healthy, happy and productive person are related to the core attachment capabilities which are formed in infancy and early childhood.[4]

In his best-selling novel *The Five People You Meet in Heaven*, Mitch Albom tells a story about the Blue Man. The Blue Man (as he was billed by the traveling carnival) had a plight that is all too common: The essence of who he was—his identity—was cursed and belittled when he was young.

The Blue Man was christened with the name Joseph Corvelzchik. When Joseph's family emigrated from Poland to America in 1894, his father took a job sewing buttons on coats in a sweatshop. As a little boy, Joseph worked in the button factory alongside his father.

One day Joseph dropped a bucket of buttons on the factory floor, only to be confronted by the foreman who began cursing him as a worthless boy. Gripped with fear and shame, Joseph soiled his pants in front of his father and the other workers. This accident brought public shame upon Joseph's father. The tension between father and son grew, and Joseph began a nighttime ritual of bed-wetting from then on. One day his father saw him when he was washing his soiled bed sheets, and Joseph later said: "He saw the dirty sheets, and then glared at me with eyes that I will never forget, as if he wished he could snap the cord of life between us."[5]

Joseph began reacting to the shame and guilt he was experiencing at home. He consulted a chemist, who prescribed silver nitrate to calm his nerves. Joseph was unknowingly drinking poison. Naturally, the prescribed doses of nitrate had no effect on his nerves, so Joseph began taking double and triple doses. It was not long before his skin turned the color of ash, then gray and finally blue. The only job Joseph could get was with a carnival that hired him as a sideshow freak. It was during his life as a professional freak that Joseph was given his name: The Blue Man.

> The "show" was simple. I would sit on the stage, half undressed, as people walked past and the barker told them how pathetic I was. For this, I was able to put a few coins in my pocket. The manager once called me the "best freak" in his stable, and, sad as it sounds, I took pride in that. When you are an outcast, even a tossed stone can be cherished.[6]

Have you ever felt like the Blue Man? Has the "cord of life" between you and the ones ordained to nurture and protect you snapped? This is a fictitious story, but I am amazed at how often life imitates art. It is absolutely true that, when the umbilical cord to our souls has been severed, we will seek out someone—anyone—who will give us an identity and name. Maybe you are like the Blue Man. Maybe you have tried to find identity by joining one of life's sideshows, but ended up feeling like someone else's property.

You were not always a freak. The poisonous venom of a cursing tongue may have slowly penetrated your emotions as you watched your true self turn ashen, gray and then blue. The Scriptures teach us:

> No man can tame the tongue. It is an unruly evil, full of deadly poison. With it we bless our God and Father, and with it we curse men, who have been made in the similitude of God.
>
> James 3:8–9

Listen to how the Message translation renders this passage: "The tongue runs wild, a wanton killer. With our tongues we bless God our Father; with the same tongues we curse the very men and women he made in his image." The pop song about someone "killing me softly with his song" may be more real than we think!

When in our developmental years we hear abusive speech like "You are worthless" or "You were a mistake," we grow to believe it. When we know only silence, our loved ones never affirm us, never express care or concern for us, we are crippled into believing that we are fundamentally unlovable and must make it on our own.

Then, with our identities shattered, we hang on to the dim hope that someday we may find a way out of the environment that is taking potshots at our souls. But once an identity is gone, shame soon enters and we begin to spend time with those who share our same sad stories. Then comes the final blow, the accusation that denies both our identities and our destinies: "You have no purpose; you are just like the crowd you run with."

It is sad but true that the home is the most dangerous environment many children will ever experience. Male children learn to mimic cursing and abusive behavior, while female children grow to believe that abuse is a normal part of family relationships. Perhaps you are even now in a verbally abusive relationship.

Let me ask you a question. Do you know your name? Not the one on your birth certificate and not the one you have come to believe in, but your *real* name—your true identity. Certainly it is not the "Blue Man." We pick up these secondhand identities in life's sideshows, but they are powerless to define our true selves, give us purpose or even offer solace to the shame that fills our souls.

Your true name, your true identity is the one that God your Father gave to you.

Changing Your Name

No, I am not talking about changing your given name. Going from Blue Man back to his christened name would not have healed the wounds of Joseph Corvelzchik. What I am speaking about is much different. I want you to receive the name—the identity—that God the Father has given you.

We find in the Scriptures that God often renamed people, aligning their names with their identities and destinies in Him. Here are some examples.

When God made a covenant with Abraham, He changed his name:

> When Abram was ninety-nine years old, the LORD appeared to Abram and said to him, "I am Almighty God; walk before Me and be blameless. And I will make My covenant between Me and you, and will multiply you exceedingly." Then Abram fell on his face, and God talked with him, saying: "As for Me, behold, My covenant is with you, and you shall be a father of many nations. No longer shall your name be called Abram, but your name shall be Abraham; for I have made you a father of many nations."
>
> Genesis 17:1–5

His given name, *Abram*, meant "exalted father." But God's purpose for Abram was much broader, and so He gave him a new name that spoke more clearly of his call, destiny and identity. *Abraham* means "father of a multitude." Imagine being 99 years old, married to a ninety-year-old woman who had never borne children, and being given the name "Father of a multitude"!

God brought Abraham's wife into the covenant relationship as well when He changed her name:

> Then God said to Abraham, "As for Sarai your wife, you shall not call her name Sarai, but Sarah shall be her

name. And I will bless her and also give you a son by her; then I will bless her, and she shall be a mother of nations; kings of peoples shall be from her."

Genesis 17:15–16

Sarai means "bitter," but *Sarah* means "beautiful mother of princes." Every time Abraham and Sarah heard their names, it reminded them of God's covenant promise and their true identities in Him.

We have discussed how Jacob deceived his elder brother and his father in order to get the birthright blessing. Because their father showed favoritism to Esau, Jacob succumbed to a lifestyle of deception—but this is not who he really was. God had greater plans for Jacob and changed his name accordingly:

So He said to him, "What is your name?" He said, "Jacob." And He said, "Your name shall no longer be called Jacob, but Israel; for you have struggled with God and with men, and have prevailed."

Genesis 32:27–28

Jacob means "supplanter" or "deceiver," but *Israel* means "prince with God."

Jesus changed Peter's name. Let's take a few moments to look at this story in more detail. Here are the words of Christ at His first encounter with the fisherman apostle: "Now when Jesus looked at him, He said, 'You are Simon the son of Jonah. You shall be called Cephas' (which is translated, A Stone)" (John 1:42).

Simon means "reed." It suggested a thin reed that grew naturally along the banks of the Sea of Galilee. These reeds bent and vacillated easily whenever the wind blew, and Simon was much like that, bending any way the wind was blowing. But Jesus saw beyond Simon's current instability and spoke about his true identity by naming him Cephas—Stone. (The name *Peter* comes from the Greek word *petros*, which means "rock.")

Jesus knew that Peter's destiny was to be a foundation stone in the early beginnings of His Church. Notice what Jesus said here: "You shall be called Cephas." In other words, "I am naming you now what you shall become." No wonder Peter was willing to lay his life down for Jesus! If someone told me that I would no longer be the Blue Man, I would follow him to the ends of the earth as well.

Yes, Peter had his struggles in changing from a reed to a stone, but Jesus later said that His Church would be built upon the foundation-stone revelation that Peter had of the divinity of Jesus.

> When Jesus came into the region of Caesarea Philippi, He asked His disciples, saying, "Who do men say that I, the Son of Man, am?" So they said, "Some say John the Baptist, some Elijah, and others Jeremiah or one of the prophets." He said to them, "But who do you say that I am?" Simon Peter answered and said, "You are the Christ, the Son of the living God." Jesus answered and said to him, "Blessed are you, Simon Bar-Jonah, for flesh and blood has not revealed this to you, but My Father who is in heaven. And I also say to you that you are Peter, and on this rock I will build My church, and the gates of Hades shall not prevail against it."
>
> Matthew 16:13–18

As he moved further still into his future destiny, Peter's rock-like identity was recognized. He was considered a pillar in the Church, for instance, and served on the apostolic council that perceived the evangelistic calling upon the life of Paul and Barnabas:

> And when James, Cephas, and John, who seemed to be pillars, perceived the grace that had been given to me

[Paul], they gave me and Barnabas the right hand of fellowship, that we should go to the Gentiles and they to the circumcised.

Galatians 2:9

It is said that when Peter was martyred for his faith in Jesus that he was crucified upside down at his own request. He simply did not feel worthy to die in the same manner as his Savior. It is also said that at the same time they were nailing Peter's hands to his cross, they were also crucifying his wife nearby. As they dropped the post of Peter's cross into the earth, and he hung upside down, he cried out in agony to his wife: "Remember Christ!"

Rock-like identity indeed. A fulfillment of destiny; recaptured passion; a severed umbilical cord healed—a Blue Man changed forever by the words "You shall be called Rock" (see John 1:42).

To each and every one of us Jesus gives a new name, a new identity and a new destiny. When you can tune out the host of confusing, competing voices long enough to hear the voice of a loving Father who is day and night speaking a new name and destiny over your future, you will become exactly the person God has ordained you to be.

Each one of us has his own gifts and callings, so each name is different. Can you doubt that He who named every star in the heavens can also call His children by name? It is this name and identity with which Jesus will greet us when we meet Him face to face:

"He who has an ear, let him hear what the Spirit says to the churches. To him who overcomes I will give some of the hidden manna to eat. And I will give him a white stone, and on the stone a new name written which no one knows except him who receives it."

Revelation 2:17

In biblical days, jurors cast white stones into urns to signify the innocence of a person on trial. Through Jesus we have been acquitted from the shame of all sin and have been given a fresh start with a new identity. The FBI's witness protection program pales in comparison.

Dear one, it is time that you look past the way others have rejected your true identity and find security in what the Father says that you will become.

> Coming to Him as to a living stone, rejected indeed by men, but chosen by God and precious, you also, as living stones, are being built up a spiritual house, a holy priesthood, to offer up spiritual sacrifices acceptable to God through Jesus Christ. Therefore it is also contained in the Scripture, "Behold, I lay in Zion a chief cornerstone, elect, precious, and he who believes on Him will by no means be put to shame."
>
> 1 Peter 2:4–6

Yes, like Peter, you and I are called in this life to be living stones—building blocks in the Church of the living Lord. And one day in the future we will be known as rock-like pillars in heaven:

> "He who overcomes, I will make him a pillar in the temple of My God, and he shall go out no more. I will write on him the name of My God and the name of the city of My God, the New Jerusalem, which comes down out of heaven from My God. And I will write on him My new name."
>
> Revelation 3:12

Finding Your Promised Name

In an age where there seems to be more cursing than blessing, along comes Jesus—the restorer of the human personality. He approaches blue men and women filled with worthlessness, shame and bitterness of soul, and speaks the words *No longer!* No longer will you be called "bitter"—now you will be called "beautiful." No longer will you be called "deceiver"—now you will be called "prince with God." No longer will you be called "reed"— now you will be called "stone."

We looked at the Aaronic blessing earlier, but I would like for us to look at it again to see a beautiful picture:

> And the LORD spoke to Moses, saying: "Speak to Aaron and his sons, saying, 'This is the way you shall bless the children of Israel. Say to them: "The LORD bless you and keep you; the LORD make His face shine upon you, and be gracious to you; the LORD lift up His countenance upon you, and give you peace."' So they shall put My name on the children of Israel, and I will bless them."
>
> Numbers 6:22–27

Did you catch it? Remember that when we were first born the umbilical cords to our souls—our human emotions—were the shining, nurturing faces of our mothers. Now notice that when God blesses us He does so by making "His face shine upon" us and "lifting up His countenance upon" us as well. In so doing He gives us peace and calms our inner beings. You might say then that the ultimate umbilical cord into our souls is the shining, nurturing face of God Himself!

Beloved, *this* cord will never be severed. God's love is unconditional. Is it any wonder that David prayed, "Do not hide Your face from me" (Psalm 102:2)? He could not bear even thinking about life without the shining face of his heavenly Father penetrating his soul. To David, the shining face of God was a symbol of mercy and salvation: "Restore us, O LORD God of hosts; cause Your face to shine, and we shall be saved!" (Psalm 80:19).

At the end of the Aaronic blessing, God the Father gives us a remarkable promise: "So they shall put My name on the children of Israel, and I will bless them" (Numbers 6:27). When we receive His covenant blessing, God places His own name upon our lives. Talk about a new identity! A quick glance at some of the Hebrew names of God will enrich your understanding of God's unconditional love for you:

Jehovah-Jireh—I Am the Lord Who Provides
Jehovah-Rapha—I Am the Lord Who Heals
Jehovah-Nissi—I Am the Lord Your Banner
Jehovah-M'Kaddesh—I Am the Lord Who Sanctifies
Jehovah-Shalom—I Am the Lord Your Peace
Jehovah-Rohi—I Am the Lord Your Shepherd
Jehovah-Shammah—I Am the Lord Who Is There
Jehovah-Tsidkenu—I Am the Lord Your Righteousness

God has honored us by calling us His own and naming us with His wonderful name.

I have often found myself condemning the twelve disciples for their childish arguments and the way they pushed and vied for position in their relationship with Jesus. Don't you find it ironic that twelve blue men, each with his own baggage and dead-end destiny, could argue over who would be the greatest? Those blue men never had any hope of getting out of the little fishing village of Capernaum, and now they wanted to fight over how many sick people they were going to heal, how many dead people they were going to raise, how many nations they were going to shake. They even resorted, in their immaturity, to quibbling over who would sit closest to Christ in His heavenly Kingdom. But these men had been with Jesus, and He successfully spoke new life into who they really were. It just took the disciples a while to compose themselves after they received the spoken blessing of a new identity, a new name and a new destiny.

As you grow in this understanding yourself, you, too, will see changes in your outlook and destiny. I will have much more to say on this subject, but first I want to give you background on how curses may have worked in your life. As you understand more the damage that has been done, you will better understand how God is working to heal and restore your wounded soul.

In the next chapter we will see how a spoken curse can last for generations. Even if you did not suffer directly from spoken curses, you could be the recipient of generational fallout that is just as deadly.

Take heart—in coming chapters we will find not only hope for the generational wounds caused by destructive tongues or destructive silence, but healing as well.

4

The Iniquity of the Fathers

Generational Fallout

"The LORD, the LORD God, merciful and gracious, longsuffering, and abounding in goodness and truth, keeping mercy for thousands, forgiving iniquity and transgression and sin, by no means clearing the guilty, visiting the iniquity of the fathers upon the children and the children's children to the third and the fourth generation."

Exodus 34:6–7

There are four elements to every story: The setting, the conflict, the climax, and the resolution. Everyone likes a good story and, when it really comes down to it, our lives are like stories. We even say things like, "That's the story of my life." Most of us wonder how our stories will end—in triumph or in tragedy. And our biggest question is probably: Will we be all alone when we take our last breath, or will we be surrounded by those who love us?

But what about the fourth and most important element in a storyline? Will we have resolved our issues, healed our wounds and helped our children to grow up without the pain and baggage that we endured? Or will we simply never complete our life's story and die with unresolved conflicts, leaving the generation that follows to unpack the bags that they inherited from us?

At the most fundamental level, the patterns of our life stories are all the same. We start our stories in a setting; we were all born into a family of some kind. Because the setting has people in it, there is always potential conflict. Conflict that is managed is healthy; unresolved conflict is destructive.

Thus, we develop our character, personality and conflict styles in the settings in which we are raised. If we are raised in a healthy environment that is filled with love, acceptance, forgiveness, mutual respect and openness, chances are pretty good that we will become well-balanced adults on our way to a storybook ending. We will leave in our wake children and grandchildren who are emotionally well-balanced and can now start their own stories, free from having to rewrite the tragedies that we left for them.

If, however, our caregivers never resolved their own life issues, they simply unpack the baggage from *their* caregivers and pile it onto us.

Someone once said that "our stories become us." The tragedy of this statement is that it is a reality for so many. Generation after generation, people live out someone else's story and come to life's end without final resolution to their conflicts. As a result, the curtain never closes on the stage, and generation after generation must deal with the same issues.

The Bible has a name for those unending tragic stories. In the Scriptures they are called generational iniquities. Look again at one of our opening verses:

"Keeping mercy for thousands, forgiving iniquity and transgression and sin, by no means clearing the guilty, visiting the iniquity of the fathers upon the children and the children's children to the third and the fourth generation."

Exodus 34:7

Notice that actions requiring forgiveness are broken down into three areas: "iniquity, transgression and sin." Sin means missing God's standard; transgression is a willful stepping aside from God's law; iniquity is often caused by a bruise from the past that has festered and is now spoiling our purpose and destiny. These bruises cause us to lose self-control in certain areas of our lives. Please note that it is *iniquity* that is passed down from one generation to the next.

It is interesting that psychologists who study the impact of unresolved family conflicts that pass from one generation to the next have a name for these unending stories. They classify unresolved family conflicts as trans-generational verbal abuse. In her book entitled *Verbal Abuse*, Dr. Grace Ketterman explains that verbal abuse is learned:

In order to survive it with even a shell of strength and some degree of personal worth, you had to master it yourself. The sad part of that process was its inevitability being passed on like a legacy to the next generation.[7]

Listen to what other leading authorities say about trans-generational abuse:

There are three primary themes that have been observed in abusive and neglectful families. The most common effect is that maltreated children are, essentially, rejected. Children that are rejected by their parents will have a host of problems including difficulty developing emotional

49

intimacy. In abusive families, it is common for this rejection and abuse to be trans-generational. The neglectful parent was neglected as a child. They pass on the way they were parented.[8]

Child abuse and neglect is trans-generational; the probability depending upon the type and extent. Comparing physical abuse to verbal abuse, verbal abuse is most likely to be transmitted from one generation to another. The form [of abuse] that is most damaging to a child's self-perception is verbal abuse.[9]

Both physical and verbal violence appear to be trans-generational.[10]

What exactly is verbal abuse? Simply put, verbal abuse is any statement, spoken or implied, that causes emotional damage. This abuse becomes trans-generational when a damaged person continues in the same storyline and carries on the abuse he or she received by imparting it to others.

Youth, like pristine glass, absorbs the prints of its handlers. Some parents smudge, others crack, a few shatter childhoods completely into jagged little pieces, beyond repair.[11]

Here is another of Dr. Ketterman's observations:

The tragedy of abuse is its repetitive pattern through succeeding generations and over a broad range of life situations. Children who were verbally abused are more than likely to abuse their peers, siblings, and teachers. As they mature, they will probably abuse their spouses, fellow employees, or bosses. If these victims are in a position of authority, they will no doubt abuse those whom they supervise. And heaven help their own children![12]

There are many forms of trans-generational verbal abuse, but my research across a wide range of studies shows me that the most common elements are:

1. Degrading (Minimizing the worth and value of another person through casting shame and ridicule)
2. Terrorizing (Threatening physical harm if expectations are not met; removing the safety of unconditional love and acceptance out of a relationship)
3. Exploiting (Modeling and mentoring control, manipulation and power over the will of another for the abuser's own benefit)
4. Rejecting (Closing the door and pulling the shade of relationship with another in order to gain a temporary sense of power and control)
5. Corrupting (Accusing another of behaviors with low value to the point that the person begins to act them out. If a young girl is called a whore long enough she may well become one.)
6. Isolating (Separating a person from social interaction with others; gaining a sense of power through the confinement and boundaries placed on another)
7. Neglecting (Overlooking and minimizing the most basic of life needs: health care, emotional needs and educational needs)

Why the Wounds Don't Heal

Perhaps the experience of reading these words about trans-generational abuse has been painful for you. Perhaps you yourself are a victim, and these first four chapters in our study feel like peeling an onion one layer at a time. Maybe you identify with Lea from chapter 2, and you are crying out, "Me, too—someone please bless me, too!" Maybe you are like the Blue Man of chapter 3, and you long to change your name. Maybe you are the child of an emotionally wounded individual and you feel as though you have taken up the impact of his or her pain. If this is true, I think it is safe for me to say that you are reading this book because you are dealing with some generational wounds.

The pathway toward healing our generational wounds starts by recognizing that the things that have happened to us are not the last word on who we are. Identifying the fact that we are victims of emotional and verbal abuse will leave us with a victim's mentality if we stay there. True healing begins when we recognize that we may have unknowingly unpacked the baggage of unresolved generational issues and are wearing someone else's costume—playing out the same dreadful drama.

You see, healing trans-generational abuse takes more than simply identifying and renouncing a bondage or iniquity that has been left for you to contend with. A costume change in the middle of a play does not change the storyline. In our rush to be free and get back on stage and bring a happy ending to our lives, we quickly sew new garments for ourselves—but this does not remove the feelings of rejection or shame. Our clothing is not unlike the fabric in Jesus' parable: "No one sews a piece of unshrunk cloth on an old garment; or else the new piece pulls away from the old, and the tear is made worse" (Mark 2:21).

Thus, it is not enough to identify and renounce these trans-generational curses or even to forgive our abusers; the curses will continue to hurt us. This is because trans-generational curses do not strike randomly; they are caused. Proverbs 26:2 states: "Like a flitting sparrow, like a flying swallow, so a curse without cause shall not alight." It may seem unfair to the innocent victim, but a curse that comes through the constant degrading, rejection and manipulation of an abuser has a cause.

A passage from James' discussion about the tongue is appropriate here:

> And the tongue is a fire, a world of iniquity. The tongue is so set among our members that it defiles the whole body, and sets on fire the course of nature; and it is set on fire by hell.
>
> James 3:6

James makes it clear that the tongue is filled with iniquity. Can it be that it is a cursing tongue that opens a porthole for iniquity to flow in from one generation to the next? This passage from 1 Peter confirms it:

> Finally, all of you be of one mind, having compassion for one another; love as brothers, be tenderhearted, be courteous; not returning evil for evil or reviling for reviling, but on the contrary blessing, knowing that you were called to this, that you may inherit a blessing. For "He who would love life and see good days, let him refrain his tongue from evil, and his lips from speaking deceit."
>
> 1 Peter 3:8–10

Each of us has a choice to speak life or death into the next generation. "A wholesome tongue," says Proverbs 15:4, "is a tree of life." Proverbs 18:21 says, "Death and life are in the power of the tongue, and those who love it will eat its fruit." You see, spoken words are like the fruit of a tree—of either blessing or cursing—that either nourishes or poisons future generations.

Physical abuse and emotional abuse are often connected and both are deeply traumatic, but note this statement from one of our earlier quotes: "The form [of abuse] that is most damaging to a child's self-perception is verbal abuse." I think that the most telling proverb concerning the tongue is this one: "There is one who speaks like the piercings of a sword, but the tongue of the wise promotes health" (Proverbs 12:18). The injuries from words pierce like a sword.

And they do not heal on their own. Though a person can be freed from a curse, and even forgive her abuser, she is still left with a gaping wound. She is still desperate for verbal blessing and acceptance. Not knowing how to fill the void, she will often return to the abuser and try once again to gain verbal blessing and love. But the abuser may not have found his or her own healing yet, and the victim gradually falls prey once again to the abuser's influence. Before long it is the same old story, same stage, same baggage—same wardrobe.

Scripture helps us understand why this crisis is so prevalent in the world today. First of all, remember from Exodus 34:7 that the "iniquity of the fathers" is passed from generation to generation. We saw that *iniquity* means a lack of self-control or "life without boundaries." The Latin root of the word *iniquity* is *in quus*, which means "harmful." Generational iniquity, then, is one generation without self-control, bruising and harming the coming generation.

As iniquity is passed down, a new generation is stripped of its protective covering and is, in turn, bruised. Left uncovered and rejected by the previous generation, this new generation loses its self-control—the inner equilibrium that balances out behaviors and life decisions. The full outworking of iniquity is found here: a life without boundaries or self-control; in a word, *lawlessness*.

The Bible tells us that in the last days a spirit of lawlessness will prevail in our world: "For the mystery of lawlessness is already at work" (2 Thessalonians 2:7).

You see, our generation is under a general curse— the curse of fatherlessness. This is not a new phenomenon. Two thousand years ago Paul the apostle said: "For though you might have ten thousand instructors in Christ, yet you do not have many fathers" (1 Corinthians 4:15). Paul was saying that, in his day, not many people were willing to have the spirit of a father and provide covering for—or mentor—others. And fatherlessness was not even a new phenomenon in Paul's day; four hundred years earlier, the Old Testament ended with a solemn warning about the true spirit of a father. Listen to the last 31 words of the Old Testament: "And he will turn the hearts of the fathers to the children, and the hearts of the children to their fathers, lest I come and strike the earth with a curse" (Malachi 4:6).

God has always designed to work across generations. He is the God of Abraham, Isaac and Jacob. Abraham, the first in God's family, was called to cover, bless and protect his son Isaac. Isaac was responsible to bless the generation that would come after him. That is the divine order of things! Each generation is to nourish and protect the following generation.

Who Is Covering You?

In 1 Corinthians 11, Paul gives us wonderful teaching about the principle of *covering*. He says in verse 3: "I want you to know that the head of every man is Christ, the head of woman is man, and the head of Christ is God." Paul is saying that every person needs a covering. Christ Himself is covered by God the Father. Men are covered by Christ, and women are covered by men. The calling and gifts of men and women are equal, but some of their roles are different. The role of the man is that of a protective covering.

One of the major aspects of spiritual covering is to make a hedge or a fence of protection around someone who is valued and loved. This helps explain a strange verse in this passage of Scripture about covering: "For this reason the woman ought to have a symbol of authority on her head, because of the angels" (1 Corinthians 11:10). What does that mean?

In that culture of that day, women prayed with their heads covered. This symbolized the fact that they were covered spiritually by male authority, which was, in turn, meant to be in submission to Christ. In other words, without their spiritual covering, women were left unprotected and vulnerable to the attack of fallen angels.

This brings us back to the curse of fatherlessness that our generation suffers. Proverbs 17:6 says that "the glory of children is their father." Today it is not at all unusual to be speaking to a group of ten people and find that eight of them are fatherless. There is further tragedy in the fact that their fathers were also rejected by *their* fathers.

And what about the women in our generation that these men are responsible for covering spiritually? They often struggle with issues of vulnerability; some resort to verbal abuse themselves, further wounding their children. Please note that I am not saying that every broken home is the fault of the husband; my point here, in the light of a fatherless culture, is that much of the anger and bitterness women feel and pass to the next generations comes as a result of lost biblical covering.

If children, in turn, are left uncovered by their parents they will naturally cover themselves. It is human nature. When children live in the shame of being fatherless—or motherless—they gradually begin to build a tower of self-preservation and self-protection. They realize that they have no one to protect them, so they begin the lifelong task of protecting themselves. In addition, a person who feels worthless and shamed has a difficult time trusting that a Father in heaven loves him. The words of Jesus in

Matthew 24:12 have come true: "And because iniquity shall abound, the love of many shall wax cold" (KJV). Dear one, please hear me, because this is crucial. When we are scarred and bruised by the baggage of a previous generation, our natural defense is to find some kind of covering to place over our wounds. But no matter how we try to cover ourselves, we will never gain enough security. Our self-made covering is just too small. Uncovered people often believe in the subtle lie that if they can stand on their own, their self-sufficiency will cover and protect them. Isaiah 28 talks about the inadequacy of people who trust in themselves and not in God. Verse 20 is a fitting commentary on our generation: "For the bed is too short to stretch out on, and the covering so narrow that one cannot wrap himself in it."

This is the conflict in our souls. Because the iniquity of past generations has bruised us and left us uncovered, the adversary of our souls would like us to believe that we can succeed in covering ourselves. But what we do not realize is that a self-made covering is actually the mantle of the adversary himself, who falsely promises to protect us and satisfy our every need.

Scripture talks about the original mantle of the enemy in Ezekiel 28. In this chapter, God is speaking about the purpose for which He created Lucifer:

"You were the anointed cherub who covers; I established you; you were on the holy mountain of God; you walked back and forth in the midst of fiery stones. You were perfect in your ways from the day you were created, till iniquity was found in you. By the abundance of your trading you became filled with violence within, and you sinned; therefore I cast you as a profane thing out of the mountain of God; and I destroyed you, O covering cherub, from the midst of the fiery stones."

Ezekiel 28:14–16

Satan's created purpose was to be the covering cherub. Yes, he was heaven's choir director and worship leader, but his main role was to cover and protect the other angels under his charge. Is it any wonder that when he fell into iniquity one third of the angels fell into iniquity with him? He had covered and influenced them. He was filled with verbal violence and imparted that to many who were under his covering. Today our adversary continues on this pathway of verbal violence. In Revelation he is called "the accuser of our brethren" (Revelation 12:10).

False and True Coverings

Two kingdoms battle for control of this world: The conflict is over who will cover the souls of men. This is a cosmic struggle and it began for man in the Garden of Eden. There Satan approached Eve with the enticing idea that if she ate of the forbidden fruit she would "be like God" (Genesis 3:5). This proposition was the original cornerstone in the tower-like prison of self-sufficiency that man has been building ever since.

We generally blame Eve for the Fall, but tell me: Where was her husband during her conversation with the enemy? Adam failed to cover his wife spiritually and protect her from temptation by reminding her of what God had actually said. Alone and uncovered, Eve fell and Adam soon followed. What happened next was remarkable: "Then the eyes of both of them were opened, and they knew that they were naked; and they sewed fig leaves together and made themselves coverings" (Genesis 3:7).

Adam and Eve had been stripped of a covering of innocence by the iniquitous tongue of the adversary. He was like an abusive father who passed down his iniquity to them, leaving them to try to cover themselves. Yes, Satan is likened to a father in the Scriptures. Listen to the words of Jesus in a conversation with the Pharisees:

"You are of your father the devil, and the desires of your father you want to do. He was a murderer from the beginning, and does not stand in the truth, because there is no truth in him. When he speaks a lie, he speaks from his own resources, for he is a liar and the father of it."

John 8:44

There is something very telling about the fig leaf garments that Adam and Eve sewed together in order to cover themselves. When they heard God walking in the garden they hid themselves, and when God called out to Adam, here is his reply: "I heard Your voice in the garden, and I was afraid because I was naked; and I hid myself" (Genesis 3:10). But wait! Adam was not naked and neither was Eve. They had already sewn fig leaves together and made coverings for themselves, so why did Adam say, "I was afraid because I was naked"?

Adam was clothed with fig leaves, but he was living the shame of the nakedness of iniquity. You see, our self-made fig robes can never cover the shame of nakedness. Self-sufficiency is only an illusion; an illusion that keeps us hiding and isolated from God's presence.

When our loving Father God "found out" what had happened, and how his first two children had come under Satan's false covering, He did a wonderful thing: "Also for Adam and his wife the LORD God made tunics of skin, and clothed them" (Genesis 3:21). It is believed that God sacrificed a lamb that day in order to make lamb's wool coverings for his children. Adam and Eve found that God's clothing provided better warmth and covering than their own fig leaves.

And the same is true for you. If you have been stripped of your covering through abuse and neglect, your fig leaves of self-sufficiency will never keep you warm—but the covering offered by the Lamb of God will be sufficient for all of your hurts and needs.

Look, for instance, at the story of the man of the Gadarenes who was tormented by a legion of demons:

> Then they sailed to the country of the Gadarenes, which is opposite Galilee. And when He [Jesus] stepped out on the land, there met Him a certain man from the city who had demons for a long time. And he wore no clothes, nor did he live in a house but in the tombs . . . and was driven by the demon into the wilderness.
>
> Luke 8:26–27, 29

Somehow, at some point in this man's life, he opened the door to the adversary's workings. Perhaps he was uncovered and began building a tower of protection. Perhaps he believed the lie of the enemy, that if he came underneath his mantle of covering his wounds would be healed. It is interesting to see what happened to this man when he allowed Satan to cover him. Not one of Satan's empty promises came true. This poor man had lived in the city, but now lived in isolation in a wilderness place. He wore no clothes, and did not have even the roof of a house to cover him!

The covering of self-preservation leads only to self-isolation and difficulty developing any warmth of intimacy with God and others. Indeed, "the bed is too short to stretch out on, and the covering so narrow that one cannot wrap himself in it."

There is a wonderful ending, however, to the story about this man of the Gadarenes. After he was set free from the destructive influence of the demons, "they went out to see what had happened, and came to Jesus, and found the man from whom the demons had departed, sitting at the feet of Jesus, clothed and in his right mind" (Luke 8:35).

He was sitting at the feet of Jesus! Remember that one of the root meanings of the word *blessing* is to "bend the knee." When one person sat at the feet of another in biblical days, he was really bending his knee in order to have hands laid on him and be blessed. The passage gives us a wonderful picture of this man, now fully clothed and covered, in the position to receive a verbal blessing from Jesus.

When we come to Jesus He never fails to cover us, renew our minds and speak words of comfort and blessing over us.

The cosmic conflict to cover men's souls began in the book of Genesis, the beginning of man's story. In the last book of the Bible, the book of Revelation, God is still pleading with uncovered men and women everywhere to allow Him to be their covering: "I counsel you to buy from Me gold refined in the fire, that you may be rich; and white garments, that you may be clothed, that the shame of your nakedness may not be revealed" (Revelation 3:18).

There is a wonderful promise for the brokenhearted in the book of Isaiah, at the heart of the Bible:

> "To console those who mourn in Zion, to give them beauty for ashes, the oil of joy for mourning, the garment of praise for the spirit of heaviness." . . . Instead of your shame you shall have double honor. . . . I will greatly rejoice in the LORD, my soul shall be joyful in my God; for He has clothed me with the garments of salvation, He has covered me with the robe of righteousness, as a bridegroom decks himself with ornaments, and as a bride adorns herself with her jewels.
>
> Isaiah 61:3, 7, 10

One day God will bring resolution to this cosmic struggle, and the souls of His saints will be eternally covered.

> And I heard, as it were, the voice of a great multitude, as the sound of many waters and as the sound of mighty thunderings, saying, "Alleluia! For the Lord God Omnipotent reigns! Let us be glad and rejoice and give Him glory, for the marriage of the Lamb has come, and His wife has made herself ready." And to her it was granted to be arrayed in fine linen, clean and bright, for the fine linen is the righteous acts of the saints.
>
> Revelation 19:6–8

Regardless of the setting and conflict of your life's story, this very moment can be the climax—the moment when you make the choice to seek healing for the transgenerational iniquity that has wounded your life. This will lead you, in turn, to a holy resolution.

The pages that follow in this book are going to take you to a point of decision in the story of your life. Will you allow your Father in heaven to clothe you and cover your shame? In your desperation for someone to bless you, will you depend on your heavenly Father who has caused His face to shine upon you and given you His own name? Can you, at this moment, come to a place where the strength of your identity no longer relies on what your abusers think about you? Can you let go of your dependence on their verbal blessing—words that may never come? Please do not keep reading from *their* script and miss the climactic moment of your own story!

You may have spent a lifetime agonizing over these issues; perhaps you have even become an abuser yourself—and now you see the resulting iniquity replaying itself in your children's stories. Maybe you became your abuser's story and your descendants are becoming yours.

I am not condemning you, only encouraging you to realize that it is never too late to bring resolution and turn your story toward an ending of peace. Generational iniquity can stop right here with you!

How do I know? In our next chapter I am going to share with you about one uncovered person's journey down the ancient path of the forgotten blessing, and how it changed his life. I know every twist and turn along the ancient path that this person walked, because I was the uncovered person.

※ 5 ※

I Won't Let You Go
Unless You Bless Me

God's Plan for Your Journey

And He said, "Let Me go, for the day breaks." But [Jacob]
said, "I will not let You go unless You bless me!"

Genesis 32:26

As we have noted, everyone has a story to tell. Somewhere
in our life experiences we find a common theme that
ties the storyline together, and we call this theme our life
message. The Scriptures teach us that the steps of the
righteous are ordered by the Lord (see Psalm 37:23).

I did not always understand how God works His will
in our lives. Most of the time, like many people I suppose, I just cared about surviving the day. I never saw the
beautiful pattern that God was creating with the pieces
of fabric that He was stitching together. I merely felt the

cuts and snips and pinpricks as He connected colors and patterns into the quilt that was my life message.

I have now learned that everything that happens to us happens for a reason, and we will see in coming chapters that this truth is necessary for us to understand if we are to relearn the forgotten ways of blessing. If we can move gracefully through life with the comprehension that everything that happens to us—whether painful or pleasurable—is part of God's handiwork, then our lives will take on a whole new meaning. No one will ever be able to harm us again, because we will know and understand that what they might mean for evil God will turn into good!

But that is for a future chapter. In this chapter I am going to share with you my life message. Everyone has a story to tell, and this is my story. This story is about one man's quest to find the forgotten blessing, and how it changed his life and faith when he found it in a small town on the back roads of Israel.

But before I tell you my story, let me first set the stage with a quick stop in a place called Peniel where, on a starlit night thousands of years ago, a desperate man wrestled for a blessing with none other than God Himself.

The Struggle

As I have mentioned, what I refer to as the forgotten blessing is the one that was spoken by Jacob over his two grandsons Ephraim and Manasseh. Jacob knew the value of a verbal blessing, because of the long, painful pathway that he took to gain one. On that lonesome, starlit night in a place called Peniel it was Jacob who wrestled with God. Jacob was a man who was desperate for verbal blessing. His desperation had been building for most of his life, and when it was finally his moment to receive the blessing, he was willing to wrestle all night long to secure it. Here is the description of this all-night wrestling match:

> Then Jacob was left alone; and a Man wrestled with him until the breaking of day. Now when He saw that He did not prevail against him, He touched the socket of his hip; and the socket of Jacob's hip was out of joint as He wrestled with him. And He said, "Let Me go, for the day breaks." But he said, "I will not let You go unless You bless me!" So He said to him, "What is your name?" He said, "Jacob." And He said, "Your name shall no longer be called Jacob, but Israel; for you have struggled with God and with men, and have prevailed." Then Jacob asked, saying, "Tell me Your name, I pray." And He said, "Why is it that you ask about My name?" And He blessed him there. So Jacob called the name of the place Peniel: "For I have seen God face to face, and my life is preserved." Just as he crossed over Penuel the sun rose on him, and he limped on his hip.
>
> Genesis 32:24–31

Let's review his story up to this pivotal episode in his life. The name *Jacob*, as we have seen, means "supplanter" or "deceiver." When he and his twin brother, Esau, were struggling in Rebekah's womb God said to her: "Two nations are in your womb, two peoples shall be separated from your body; one people shall be stronger than the other, and the older shall serve the younger" (Genesis 25:23). God had already determined that Esau would be born first, but would serve his younger brother. This was not customary, for the oldest son always got the birthright blessing. As the sons grew, Isaac did not heed God's word but showed favoritism to the older son. "So the boys grew. And Esau was a skillful hunter, a man of the field; but Jacob was a mild man, dwelling in

67

tents. And Isaac loved Esau because he ate of his game" (Genesis 25:27–28).

I can only imagine the heartbreak in Jacob's soul when he realized that his father loved Esau more than him. We cannot be sure whether he was motivated by jealousy or by brokenness, but we saw in chapter 2 how Jacob manipulated Esau into selling his birthright for a bowl of stew. Later Jacob covered himself in Esau's garments and goatskins to gain the birthright blessing from his blind father. All along the way Jacob was building his own tower of self-sufficiency, covering and protecting himself.

When Esau learned that Jacob had stolen the birthright blessing by deception he threatened to murder Jacob, and Jacob fled to Syria, to the home of his uncle in Padan Aram. Far from his home, living in a foreign country, Jacob pledged to work for Laban for seven years in order to gain the hand of his daughter Rachel in marriage. On the wedding day, Laban switched brides and gave his older daughter to Jacob instead of Rachel. Laban then forced Jacob to work another seven years in order to gain Rachel's hand. In all, Jacob worked for his father-in-law for twenty years.

After those many years of hard labor, Laban turned against Jacob, and Jacob fled with his wives, eleven sons and livestock. Listen to the parting conversation between Jacob and Laban:

> "These twenty years I have been with you; your ewes and your female goats have not miscarried their young, and I have not eaten the rams of your flock. That which was torn by beasts I did not bring to you; I bore the loss of it. You required it from my hand, whether stolen by day or stolen by night. There I was! In the day the drought consumed me, and the frost by night, and my sleep departed from my eyes. Thus I have been in your house twenty years; I served you fourteen years for your two

daughters, and six years for your flock, and you have changed my wages ten times."

Genesis 31:38–41

When Jacob explained to Rachel and Leah that he desired to take his family back to his own country,

Rachel and Leah answered and said to him, "Is there still any portion or inheritance for us in our father's house? Are we not considered strangers by him? For he has sold us, and also completely consumed our money."

Genesis 31:14–15

After being rejected by his father and his brother, and both deceived and rejected by his father-in-law, I can imagine that Jacob was dead serious when he said to God: "I will not let You go unless You bless me!" After Jacob received a blessing from the Lord Himself and had his name changed from *deceiver* to *Israel*, which, as we have noted, means "prince with God," he came out of the wrestling match limping on his hip. God had touched him in the place of his strength.

It would be safe to say that Jacob's wrestling match with God was also his moment of decision. It was the climactic moment in his sojourn—the moment when he was healed of the wounds that come from being rejected. It was also the moment when he set aside the building blocks he was using to construct his own tower of self-sufficiency. His struggle with God and man was over, and he was now on his way to wholeness.

Though our paths might differ, our quests for verbal blessing are just as desperate as Jacob's. My journey took me through the back roads of modern Israel, to a little town called Netziona. It was there that I came to understand that all of the snips and cuts and stitches of my life were actually contributing to a beautiful pattern I had not yet seen. It was there that I came to understand the forgotten blessing. Here is my story.

Blessings Lost and Found

I am a Jew. This is not a title that I am accustomed to acknowledging. I have rarely shared about my Jewish heritage in public and, for the most part, never thought that my genealogical roots mattered much in my profession as a pastor. Sure, I could from time to time capitalize on my heritage—a sermon about the importance of praying for the peace of Jerusalem, or a human interest story about my family's Yiddish humor. But in a sense I had forgotten about my background and could not reconcile a cultural Jewish heritage with Christian living. I have never seen my Jewish background as bringing me a richer experience in my faith, because I have always believed that, in Jesus, there is neither Jew nor Gentile, male nor female, slave nor free—for we are all one in Christ. This is true, yet I am a Jew nonetheless.

I am a Jew who, for most of his life, distanced himself from his heritage and, in many ways, forgot it. I believe that Christian churches are filled with generations of believers who are as disconnected from their heritage as I was. Why have these rich traditions been neglected and lost by the Body of Christ? A quick glance at Church history is revealing. To understand how Christians came to neglect the powerful principle of verbal blessing, you need travel no further than your local theater. It was in the theater that in recent days an age-old wound was opened once again between Christians and Jews. I am talking, of course, about Mel Gibson's 2004 movie, *The Passion of the Christ*.

Prior to the film's release, a flood of concern poured out of the Jewish community. The fear was that Jews would be depicted in a negative way, and that the world would answer with another barrage of the violent anti-Semitism that Jews have endured for thousands of years. I think that Mel Gibson portrayed the crucifixion of Christ in a powerful way, and when it came to nailing Christ's hands and feet to the cross, Mel chose to film his own hand as the one that held the nail. I did not walk away from the film with negative feelings toward Jews. I had instead a sense of brokenness over what Christ had done for me.

But this is what concerned me about the debate that preceded the release of *The Passion of the Christ*: Christian leaders were interviewed on nearly every news channel—and they could not seem to understand why Jewish people might be concerned! It was as if for a moment we completely forgot about a Church history that is filled with anti-Jewish sentiment.

Look at this brief overview. By the middle of the third century, church leaders came to believe that God was pleased when Jerusalem was destroyed and the Jews scattered across the world. Christians were deceived into thinking that it was His way of punishing the Jews for killing His Son. Origen, a church leader in the third century, wrote these words: The Jews "will never be restored to their former condition. For they have committed a crime of the most unhallowed kind, in conspiring against the Savior of the human race."

In A.D. 325 Emperor Constantine called church leaders together in a gathering known as the Nicene Council. Emperor Constantine had some issues, one of which was that he did not like Jews. He influenced the Council to separate once and for all from the traditions of the Jews and to practice them no longer. One of the facts of our Christian faith is that the resurrection of Jesus took place on Passover weekend. Yet the beautiful picture of the spotless Passover lamb being taken outside the gate of the city to be sacrificed—as Jesus was in the same hour on the same day—is now often missed by Christians.

You see, Constantine thought that celebrating the resurrection on the rightful day of Passover was making too much of a connection with Jewish tradition. The Nicene Council, in turn, moved the resurrection celebration to what they believed to be a more fitting date—the day when pagans of the Middle Ages celebrated the re-birth of spring and the patron goddess of fertility.

The name of this goddess was *Ishtar* and, if you say it out loud, it might sound familiar. *Ishtar* is the name from which we derive the modern word *Easter*. The symbol of the resurrection—Christ's empty tomb—is now often overshadowed by the fertile bunny rabbit and painted *Ishtar* eggs!

Here is what Emperor Constantine wrote about the date change:

> It appeared an unworthy thing that in the celebration of this most holy feast, we should follow the practice of the Jews, who have impiously defiled their hands with an enormous sin, and are, therefore, deservedly afflicted with blindness of soul.

After Martin Luther led the Church into reformation, he had a sincere passion to win Jewish people to Jesus. But when they would not convert, he began to despise them. Here is what he wrote in his bitterness: "They [the Jews] deserve to be hated. God hates them, and so they are hated by the Apostles and all who are of God."

It is a tragic fact that Adolph Hitler justified the massacre of six million Jews by gleaning support from Christian writers. Luther himself is quoted in Hitler's book, *Mein Kampf*! As the Jews were led to the gas chambers they were greeted by signs that read "Christ killers."

Remembering these things should make it easy for us to understand why Jews might be concerned about Christian anti-Semitism.

I mentioned earlier that, though I have Jewish roots, I always found it difficult to connect my Christian faith with anything Jewish. To be honest, I never saw the need because I did not know what I was missing. I am ashamed to admit that I never had the slightest desire to travel to the Holy Land. I once even turned down a free pastors' tour that was offered by the Israeli government. I saw no need (other than learning new geographical insights) to spend any time learning about Jewish customs. But insights have a way of changing, and stories sometimes take unexpected turns. Here is how my story began.

My great-grandmother Cilia was born in a small Jewish village in Ukraine. Her family name was Boxerman. In the early 1900s, just prior to the Bolshevik Revolution, Cilia immigrated to Canada and then to New York City. She was married to Jacob Krupnick and they owned a fur store. Cilia and Jacob eventually had two daughters, Rose and Pauline, and a son named William. William died of infection at the age of twelve. Rose was my grandmother.

After several years in New York, the family moved to the Jewish community of Venice in southern California. Jacob and Cilia lived very comfortably in the warm Mediterranean climate—a vast difference from the harsh Ukraine winters Cilia had known.

My grandmother Rose met a German young man named Max; they married and moved to Anaheim, near Los Angeles. Max had no religious background and, in fact, called himself an atheist. (That must have been an interesting combination: a traditional Jew and a German atheist!) Their first child was a son, whom they named after Rose's brother, William. William was my father.

When my father was a toddler, Rose took a Sunday afternoon walk down the sidewalks of Anaheim, and heard beautiful music coming from a nearby building. She ventured inside the large building, and heard for the first time the wonderful hymns that speak of Jesus our Savior. As she sat and listened to the music, she had a vision of Christ hanging on the cross and dying for her sins. After the singing, Rose heard the message of Jesus the Messiah articulated with love. When the altar call was given, she found her way to the front and received Jesus as her Lord.

It turned out that the building my grandmother wandered into was Angeles Temple, pastored by Amy Semple McPherson. Soon after being saved, Rose was baptized in water. We still have her baptism certificate, signed by Miss McPherson.

Imagine the shock to Rose's Jewish family when she told them of her vision and her acceptance of Jesus! The dream that led her to freedom was a nightmare for them. Her father, Jacob Krupnick, said to her: "Oh, Rose, you are my precious daughter—but I can never speak to you again. You are dead to me!"

Not long after Rose was converted, Max was radically saved as well. Born to Max and Rose were eleven children: William, Miriam, Sarah, Nathan, Joseph, Philip, Naomi, Ruth, Jacqueline, Daniel and Rachel. I can imagine that it would have been difficult for Rose to be estranged from her family while raising so many children. As the children grew, Jacob and Cilia allowed for annual visits with Rose and her children, but the relationship was difficult and the estrangement never really ended.

My father became a general contractor, married his sweetheart, Nora, had two children (my sister and me), and was full into the swing of the California building boom of the 1960s. I will never forget the night he died. He was in his early thirties.

Dad had recently purchased a new tract of land and built the first house on it, which our family was living in. He already had five more houses under construction, with more planned to start once they were finished. It was early evening, the night before Christmas Eve, and my father needed to drop some things off at our church for his Sunday school class the next morning.

I can remember wrestling with my father as he approached the front door to leave. I was three and a half years old, and I clung to his leg much as Jacob clung to God in Peniel. I remember saying, "I won't let you go, Daddy, unless you take me with you!" He reminded me that I had already had my bath and was dressed for bed, and that he would be back in a flash to read me my bedtime story just like usual. But I persisted: "I won't let you go, Daddy, unless you take me with you!"

My father weakened, took me up in his arms, and opened the door to take me along for the ride. But it was chilly outside, so he set me down and told me to stay put until he came back. He never came back. A holiday drunk driver was speeding through the streets and took my father's life as he pulled out of our subdivision.

My mother went to work full-time after my father's death and attended night school classes. I spent my early years with my grandparents. Almost all of my earliest memories are of following in the footsteps of my grandmother Rose. I was her shadow until my teenage years. Since I was the eldest son of her eldest son, I think that Rose was somehow replacing the memory of her son with me. I can remember her hand always being upon my head, either praying blessing or proclaiming blessing. At naptime I was always given the place on Rose's coveted feather bed.

I had lunch with my grandmother several times a week during my teenage years. Instead of attending the prom the night I graduated from high school, I went straight to Rose's house where, as usual, she placed her hand upon my head and blessed me.

But there was still an awful shame inside me during those formative years. It was the shame of being fatherless. I tried to cover my pain and, at thirteen, started washing dishes in a restaurant full-time in order to buy clothes like the other children's. I became self-sufficient and developed tremendous anger and resentment toward God for allowing my father to be stripped from me. You see, I spent many years building walls of self-protection and self-sufficiency, but the bed was always too short and the covering always too narrow, and I could never keep myself warm.

My grandmother often spoke to me about her estrangement with her family. There was a longing in her to be connected, cherished and loved by her Jewish family, but the estrangement and rejection continued throughout her life. I will never forget that, when Rose was near death, she called me into her bedroom and placed her hands upon my head and spoke a word of blessing over my future. She also prayed that somehow her Jewish family in California and in Tel Aviv, Israel, might come to know her Messiah, Jesus. This was the first I had ever heard of any family living in Israel, and I filed the news away in my memory bank.

Rose passed away, and I moved to Chicago to attend seminary, married and had four children of my own. I forgot about the blessings that Rose had spoken over my life. I forgot about the wonderful connection my family had always made between our Jewish heritage and our Christian faith. I forgot about the family gatherings where we sang Jewish songs, ate Jewish food and laughed about Yiddish sayings. I had become a Christian pastor; what did Jewish customs have to do with me?

But insights have a way of changing, and stories sometimes take unexpected turns. Three years ago I spoke on a series of messages entitled "The Forgotten Blessing" at the church where I am privileged to be a pastor. But even after I spoke about the power of verbal blessing I still did not make a connection with the Jewish custom of the spoken blessing and my grandmother's hand of blessing upon my head.

It was not long after I finished this series on the forgotten blessing that I was invited again to go on a pastors' trip to Israel. And, suddenly, I had a strange (for me) desire to go! I called my grandmother's sister's family before I departed, and asked them for the names and numbers of Rose's cousins who lived in Tel Aviv. My desire to find them was based purely on curiosity. I had honestly forgotten my grandmother's dying prayer, as I had forgotten everything that had any Jewish connection.

When I arrived in Tel Aviv I called my grandmother's first cousin, David. His father was my grandmother's uncle, who had emigrated from Ukraine to Israel at the same time Cilia had gone to America. In the telephone conversation I told David that I was the grandson of his cousin Rose and he asked me who Rose was. "Rose," I said, "was Pauline's sister, the daughter of Cilia."

"Pauline doesn't have a sister!" David said abruptly, sounding very surprised. He was ready to hang up on me, thinking that I was an imposter, when I began to name other members of Pauline's family. Somehow I convinced him that I was a family member of one kind or another, and he invited me to his house for the coming weekend.

When David greeted me, I was staggered at how closely he resembled my grandmother. He could have been her twin! He pulled out the book of family genealogical history more or less immediately and, there in the Hebrew language, were the names of my great-grandparents Cilia and Jacob Krupnick, their son, William, and daughter, Pauline, and Pauline's children—but no Rose!

77

David's entire Eastern-European family had died at the hands of the Nazis. During his young adult years David's only living family was his Aunt Cilia and cousin Pauline. For 35 years David had worked as the Avionics director of the Israeli airline El Al. His job was buying airplanes and airplane parts in America, and he and his children had visited Cilia many times in Los Angeles before she passed away. Yet she never told him about her daughter—his cousin Rose! The rejection was deeper than I thought.

David felt, quite understandably, that it was impossible for Rose ever to have existed. How could he be so close to his only remaining family and never have heard about a second daughter? I told him that Rose had become a Christian and had been rejected by her parents; that that was why they never told him that she was alive and had eleven children.

Still disbelieving, David called his sister, Menucha, who lived in downtown Tel Aviv. Menucha had lived with my great-grandmother Cilia while going to school at UCLA during the sixties, and David thought that perhaps she would have heard something about a daughter named Rose. He conversed with his sister in expressive Hebrew as I stared at the ceiling, wondering how I could get out of this situation gracefully before this nice man and his wife, Shoshanna, became fully convinced that I was a scam artist.

Here I was: a forty-something man who had just cancelled a morning flight in order to rent a compact (meaning *tiny*) Italian car, drive the back roads of Israel to a little village called Netziona and meet my grandmother's cousin who didn't believe in her existence.

What was I thinking? I groaned inside.

I was not on a mission to right a wrong, heal 75 years of family estrangement or fulfill Rose's dying prayer. I was a self-sufficient man who did not need intimacy or blessing for that matter. Estrangement had become a way of life for my grandmother; if she could survive being rejected and uncovered, then so could I. As a result of being fatherless, I never really came to a place of recognizing my need for other people. I learned out of necessity that I could take care of myself and, because of my tower of self-sufficiency, I had become a strict taskmaster in my home.

In fact, at this point in my life I focused on imparting to my children the self-sufficient attitude that I had developed in myself. It sounded noble to think that I was helping them grow to be mature and responsible by piling more tasks on them, but I was simply, steadily, passing on to the next generation my own bondage. Of course, I could not see it that day in Netziona. I just wanted to end the silly ordeal I had gotten myself into and get to the Ben Gurian airport in time to catch my flight to Switzerland, where I planned on having a few days to sightsee in the Alps before I returned home.

The Hebraic phone conversation had droned on long enough for me to count about a quarter of the ceiling tiles in David and Shoshanna's condo when the inflection of David's voice told me that there had been a serious shift in the discussion. Tears began to flow down his face, and I suddenly realized that I was not going to be seeing the Swiss Alps that day. In fact, in that moment I lost all interest in anything else.

Suddenly, everything came back to me: My grandmother's constant words of blessing, her hands of blessing on my head, the Jewish songs, the Jewish food, the Yiddish humor and my grandmother's dying prayer that her family in Israel would come to know her Messiah.

David looked dazed as he handed me the phone and Menucha, my newfound cousin, began telling me in broken English that for more than forty years she had kept the family secret—that Cilia had another daughter named Rose.

You know something? There comes an incredible feeling of love and acceptance when you find out that you have the right to exist—especially when you have never before felt that you had that right. Somehow in that moment, though I never experienced the rejection my grandmother endured, I felt as if I were a representative character that brought healing to the gaping wound of rejection that my entire family had endured for decades.

What happened next began a healing work in my life that continues to this day. David and Shoshanna embraced me, laid hands upon my head and spoke a verbal blessing over my life. As they covered me with words of blessing, my tower of self-sufficiency crumbled and, for the first time, I realized the incredible power of spoken words of acceptance.

I stayed another four days in the Holy Land, crisscrossing the countryside and visiting with David and his sister, Menucha. I learned many things during that momentous trip, but what impressed me the most is how very culturally Jewish it is to bless someone verbally.

On a subsequent journey to Israel, while walking down the streets of Jerusalem with my wife and a dear Israeli friend named Yisroel Stefansky, I noticed a poster in a shop window. It depicted a father laying his hands upon his children. At the bottom of the poster were words in the Hebrew language. I asked Yisroel what the words meant and he said, "These words say: 'May you be like Ephraim and Manasseh.'" The forgotten blessing! I bought the poster.

The picture of a father blessing his children is a common one in Jewish homes. On another trip to Israel, I was in a hotel meeting room with several government officials. On the other side of the hall was a large conference room that doubled as a synagogue. I saw a long line of men wearing yarmulkes, waiting for a rabbi to lay hands upon their heads. My curiosity got the best of me so I walked across the hall and asked someone what was happening. He looked at me in disbelief and said, "You don't know? Why, he's blessing them, of course!" Borrowing a yarmulke, I got in line myself. When I approached the rabbi he asked me in English: "How can I bless you today?"

I asked him to bless my four children and my wife by name, and this wonderful rabbi spoke the blessing of Ephraim and Manasseh over my life and family.

Over the last three years I have begun to practice this principle of blessing my family with the forgotten blessing, and the changes in our relationships have been astonishing. We have learned firsthand how the forgotten blessing can bring healing once and for all to the gaping wounds caused by generational verbal abuse and rejection.

My relationship with my eldest daughter, Rachel, now nineteen years of age, was very strained during her middle teenage years. Parents generally make the big mistakes with the first child and then perfect their skills on the next ones coming up. My way of handling the general teenage issues of newfound independence and autonomy in Rachel was to lash out at her verbally and declare her to be not fully committed to her parents' covering. The more I used vocabulary like *rebellious* or *stubborn* or *self-willed*, the further apart Rachel and I grew. Our relationship finally crumbled into a mass of disjointed communication and general avoidance of one another. Looking back, I see that Rachel was a very good girl. She never crossed the line in the arena of purity or morals and she was and is very spiritually connected and God-centered. She has an excellent spirit.

The problem resided in my unwillingness to trust her and in my continued verbal assault on her seemingly stubborn demeanor. Everything changed, however, when I began to understand the power of the forgotten blessing! Within one week of embracing Rachel and drawing her into my circle of love through verbal blessing, our "cold war" relationship turned into an open one of trust and mutual respect. I am certain that I will make awkward mistakes and errors in my future parenting decisions, but because of the principle of the forgotten blessing our family has an exciting future ahead—one filled with resolution and hope.

6

When God Crossed His Hands

Your Value in God's Eyes

Then Israel stretched out his right hand and laid it on Ephraim's head, who was the younger, and his left hand on Manasseh's head, guiding his hands knowingly, for Manasseh was the firstborn.

Genesis 48:14

Children need constant reinforcements of a parent's love. It does not matter how many times parents tell them that they love them, children need to hear it again. My children—ages six through nineteen—often quiz me about the degree of my love for them. If they see me in the kitchen kissing their mother they sometimes will ask: "Dad, do you love Mom more than us?" To which I reply: "Of course not! I love Mom with everything within me and I've been crazy about her ever since we met. It was love at first sight and my heart skips a beat every time she walks into the room. And do you know what? We love you with everything within us and the first day you came into our lives it was love at first sight! In fact, every time you walk into the room our hearts skip a beat."

At the end of the speech we normally do a kitchen group-hug with lots of kissing and carrying on! Another thing that I do is tell each of my kids privately that he or she is my favorite child. They know that I love every one of them equally, but it is my way of letting them know they are unique and hold a special place in their father's heart. One Valentine's Day I had an artist create an individual card for each of them. At the bottom of each card I wrote: "Don't tell your siblings, but you are my favorite." My cover was blown when at the table they compared cards!

You know, it would be funny if it were not so painfully true that we never stop questioning the degree of our parents' love for us. I have heard grown siblings say things like "You were always Mom's favorite" or "You were the apple of Dad's eye." Most of the time the comments are made in jest, but they probably ring with truth.

Just as we did while children, we grown-ups make comparisons between God's blessings on us and His blessings on others. Perhaps you have caught yourself feeling less than thrilled when a friend calls and tells you how God recently blessed him. He tells you how he burned the mortgage papers on his house, got a new job that doubled his income and, on top of that, his kid just received a full scholarship to an Ivy League school. You know that, as a Christian, you are supposed to rejoice with those who rejoice, but at the end of the conversation he says the words that push you over the edge: "God has been so good to me and I just wanted to share it with someone." And there you are, doubting that God loves you as much as He loves your friend!

Have you ever questioned the degree of love that your heavenly Father has for you? Have you ever measured the blessing He is pouring out upon you and compared it with the measure of blessing He is pouring out on someone else? Have you ever thought that God plays favorites? More specifically, have you ever assumed that God loves Jesus more than He loves you?

I do not believe that we ask these questions simply because we are jealous or greedy. What I do sense is that, just as my children want to know where they stand in my love for them, we as God's children want to know where we stand in His love for us. We want to know if we are one of His favorites or if, when asked about our welfare, He would have to fish for a while to remember our names.

The answer to these questions is found on the ancient path of the forgotten blessing, and in this chapter we are going to finish our brush-clearing project and then start walking confidently toward our destination—learning to apply verbal blessing in our lives. I am going to give you many specific guidelines concerning spoken blessing in the chapters that follow.

Remember, I warned you up front that ancient pathways have many thorns and thistles that must be cleared before we can complete the journey. Finding ancient pathways is hard work. I am thankful that you have come this far, and hope that you have not been scraped too badly by the thorns along the way.

You see, dear one, we have come through a lot of thick brush to arrive at this point. Now I am going to tie all of our stories together—yours, mine, Lea's, the Blue Man's, Jacob's—and you will see what we all have in common. Are you ready? Listen as I tell you one more story. This one is about two princes and a princess, but it is far from a fairy tale.

During the days of the patriarchs and kings, the sons and daughters of royalty wore coats of many colors. There are three people mentioned in the Scriptures by name who wore this type of garment. Each of these garments was torn or damaged in some way. But, as we will find in the pages that follow, there is beauty in the torn robe.

Tamar

Tamar was a princess, a daughter of King David. Her short story is found in 2 Samuel 13. Tamar was a beautiful girl who caught the eye of a young man named Amnon. The problem was that Amnon was her half brother. They had different mothers, but David was their father; marriage between them was impossible. Amnon was so captivated by his sister's beauty that he asked his father to send Tamar to his house to cook a meal for him. He told his father that he was ill and needed Tamar's help.

After she cooked for Amnon, he refused to eat, sent out his household servants and physically attacked his sister and raped her. Afterward, Amnon was filled with anger.

> Then Amnon hated her exceedingly, so that the hatred with which he hated her was greater than the love with which he had loved her. And Amnon said to her, "Arise, be gone!" So she said to him, "No, indeed! This evil of sending me away is worse than the other that you did to me." But he would not listen to her. Then he called his servant who attended him, and said, "Here! Put this woman out, away from me, and bolt the door behind her." Now she had on a robe of many colors, for the king's virgin daughters wore such apparel. And his servant put her out and bolted the door behind her.
> Then Tamar put ashes on her head, and tore her robe of many colors that was on her, and laid her hand on her head and went away crying bitterly. And Absalom her brother said to her, "Has Amnon your brother been

with you? But now hold your peace, my sister. He is your brother; do not take this thing to heart." So Tamar remained desolate in her brother Absalom's house.

2 Samuel 13:15–20

Notice that Tamar "remained desolate." Those two words carry both a negative and positive perspective. Tamar was desolate, but she remained! Let me just say that if there is a Tamar reading these words and the glory of your innocence has been torn from you, please remain! I am going to show you your value, the purpose for your life, the promise that awaits you. You will find peace again—your innocence will be restored, as pure as an April shower and as clean as freshly washed linen.

I live in the Gulf Coast, where palm trees grow naturally along the roadside. Palm trees are tropical plants, but are hardy and can survive a harsh freeze. I learned this one year when I failed to cover my sego palm tree during a winter cold snap. The branches were damaged by the cold, and by early spring they had decayed and were falling off. So I cut down the tree and threw it into a pile of dead leaves and shrubs. By midsummer, however, new green palm shoots were growing out of the dead leaves and, when I cleared away the debris, I found a brand-new palm tree growing happily where I had "planted" it. I should have allowed it to remain in my yard!

Tamar in Hebrew means "palm tree." This is a wonderful image. Though her beautiful coat was torn from her, she remained. Though abused and bitterly rejected, she remained. She was a "palm tree," and she survived.

Joseph

The second person in the Bible who wore the royal coat of many colors was Joseph. His father, Jacob, made

87

it for him. This coat was more than just a covering; it was a sign of honor and royalty. No one has ever come up with an exact description of what this coat looked like, but the best guess is that it was a long robe with sleeves, made from strips of different colored fabrics.

Why would Joseph, one of twelve brothers, be honored with such an excellent gift? Genesis 37:3 tells us this: "Now Israel loved Joseph more than all his children, because he was the son of his old age. Also he made him a tunic of many colors." Ten of his brothers were older in age—Benjamin, Rachel's other son, was youngest—and Joseph was probably alone with his father a great deal. Perhaps a deeper bond was established between them as a result.

Joseph was a young man in his mid-teens when he was given the coat, and could not have known the anger and jealousy that his father's affectionate gift would fuel among his brothers. Joseph wore his many-colored coat with honor. I can only imagine the verbal assaults on his character and motivations.

About this time, God in His providence began to give Joseph dreams concerning his future, and this sealed his brothers' hatred for him:

> Joseph, being seventeen years old, was feeding the flock with his brothers. . . .
>
> Now Joseph had a dream, and he told it to his brothers; and they hated him even more. So he said to them, "Please hear this dream which I have dreamed: There we were, binding sheaves in the field. Then behold, my sheaf arose and also stood upright; and indeed your sheaves stood all around and bowed down to my sheaf." And his brothers said to him, "Shall you indeed reign over us? Or shall you indeed have dominion over us?" So they hated him even more for his dreams and for his words.
>
> Then he dreamed still another dream and told it to his brothers, and said, "Look, I have dreamed another

dream. And this time, the sun, the moon, and the eleven stars bowed down to me." So he told it to his father and his brothers; and his father rebuked him and said to him, "What is this dream that you have dreamed? Shall your mother and I and your brothers indeed come to bow down to the earth before you?" And his brothers envied him, but his father kept the matter in mind.

Genesis 37:2, 5–11

The dreams would actually come true one day in the distant future but, in the meantime, they became further cause for Joseph's brothers to speak unkind words to him. I find it interesting that Joseph's dreams followed the royal covering of his father. That royal, many-colored coat was a providential sign to Joseph that God had placed a mantle of kingship upon him, and he began to walk accordingly in his newfound identity.

The jealousy in his older brothers' hearts turned from bitterness to hatred and finally to a murderous proposition. Joseph was sent by his father to check on the welfare of his brothers, who were feeding their father's flock in Shechem. When Joseph arrived in Shechem he could not find his brothers and, like a good shepherd, he wandered from field to field looking for the sheep and his brothers.

Now a certain man found him, and there he was, wandering in the field. And the man asked him, saying, "What are you seeking?" So he said, "I am seeking my brothers. Please tell me where they are feeding their flocks." And the man said, "They have departed from here, for I heard them say, 'Let us go to Dothan.'" So Joseph went after his brothers and found them in Dothan.

Genesis 37:15–17

My heart goes out to young Joseph. He was on his way to seek the well-being of his brothers who hated and ridiculed him daily, and they were not there when he arrived. There he was in Shechem, dressed in a royal coat of many colors, walking from field to field, seeking out lost sheep and lost brothers. This verse makes Joseph's attitude of servanthood in the face of rejection all the more real to me.

A man pointed Joseph in the right direction, and with the sun shining on his many-colored robe, his brothers recognized him immediately.

> Now when they saw him afar off, even before he came near them, they conspired against him to kill him. Then they said to one another, "Look, this dreamer is coming! Come therefore, let us now kill him and cast him into some pit; and we shall say, 'Some wild beast has devoured him.' We shall see what will become of his dreams!"
>
> Genesis 37:18–20

He was coming to his own, but his own would not receive him. When Joseph joined his brothers,

> they stripped Joseph of his tunic, the tunic of many colors that was on him. Then they took him and cast him into a pit. And the pit was empty; there was no water in it.
>
> Genesis 37:23–24

For some people, the family is a very dangerous place indeed!

A caravan of Midianite traders passed by not much later, and Joseph's brothers sold him as a slave for twenty pieces of silver. Talk about family rejection—these brothers wrote the textbook! To cover their crime, the brothers slaughtered a young goat and dipped Joseph's royal robe in its blood.

Then they sent the tunic of many colors, and they brought it to their father and said, "We have found this. Do you know whether it is your son's tunic or not?" And he recognized it and said, "It is my son's tunic. A wild beast has devoured him. Without doubt Joseph is torn to pieces." Then Jacob tore his clothes, put sackcloth on his waist, and mourned for his son many days.

Genesis 37:32–34

As a slave, Joseph was falsely accused and sent to prison by his master. Prison life must have been devastating to a shepherd boy from the little village of Hebron. Prisons in Egypt would have been foul-smelling and unbearably hot. And David records this in the Psalms: "He sent a man before them—Joseph—who was sold as a slave. They hurt his feet with fetters, he was laid in irons" (Psalm 105:17–18). Joseph's ankles were locked in fetters and chains. Every time he lifted his hand to wipe the sweat from his brow his clumsy chains would rattle.

The king's enemies were there—political prisoners with long histories of vice and corruption. I am sure that Joseph's days were filled with stories from the inner-workings of Egypt's government. Men who had lost power and been accused by the Pharaoh whom they served were likely filled with rage. Revenge and hatred breeds among men who have been chained to walls. Shackled together with them is young Joseph, and he spends the next ten to fifteen years hearing the cries of desperate men in the belly of the prison.

There are many people today whose lives mirror Joseph's. Not only do they suffer bitter words spoken against their identity and life dreams, but they also endure rejection from the very ones they are seeking to serve. As a result they spend years locked in a prison, shackled to lies about their identities.

Eventually Joseph was shown mercy and favor while in the prison, and he became known as one who could interpret dreams. Pharaoh had a dream about seven fat cows and seven skinny cows, and Joseph was brought out of the prison to interpret the dream. Joseph told Pharaoh that the land of Egypt was about to experience seven years of plenty. Joseph encouraged Pharaoh to store up food and grain during those seven years, because they would be followed by seven years of severe famine. After Joseph finished interpreting the dream, Pharaoh proclaimed:

> "Can we find such a one as this, a man in whom is the Spirit of God?" Then Pharaoh said to Joseph, "Inasmuch as God has shown you all this, there is no one as discerning and wise as you. You shall be over my house, and all my people shall be ruled according to your word; only in regard to the throne will I be greater than you." And Pharaoh said to Joseph, "See, I have set you over all the land of Egypt." Then Pharaoh took his signet ring off his hand and put it on Joseph's hand; and he clothed him in garments of fine linen and put a gold chain around his neck. And he had him ride in the second chariot which he had; and they cried out before him, "Bow the knee!" So he set him over all the land of Egypt.
>
> Genesis 41:38–43

Why tell you about Joseph's many-colored coat, his years in prison and his subsequent promotion? Remember that it was Joseph's two sons, born to him while he ruled in Egypt, whose lives form the basis of the forgotten blessing.

Soon after Joseph interpreted Pharaoh's dreams he was given Asenath, the daughter of Poti-Pherah, priest of On, as his wife. The boys, Ephraim and Manasseh, were born during the seven years of plenty. Their names are significant because they are really the first glimpse we get into Joseph's heart after all that had happened to him. Had the revenge and bitterness of his fellow prisoners been imparted to him during his years being incarcerated? Had he been dreaming of ways to bring his brothers to justice? With all of the verbal cursing and rejection he had endured as a child, he could have easily named his sons Bitterness of Soul and Rejection. Instead,

> Joseph called the name of the firstborn Manasseh: "For God has made me forget all my toil and all my father's house." And the name of the second he called Ephraim: "For God has caused me to be fruitful in the land of my affliction."
>
> Genesis 41:51–52

According to Strong's *Concordance*, the word *toil* means "sorrow, labor, grief, pain, trouble, misery, fatigue and exhaustion." Joseph was ridiculed and rejected, stripped of his covering of many colors that spoke of God's royal purpose in his life, thrown into an empty pit and left rotting and forgotten in a prison. Dear one, that *is* the definition of toil!

Yet Joseph said that God caused him to forget all of his toil. Not only did God cause him to forget his sorrowful labor as a slave and an inmate, but he also made him forget all of the pain of his father's house, all the things that happened to him in that setting.

I really believe that Joseph was reminded of God's restoration work every time he called the name of his firstborn, *Manasseh*, "making forgetful." And Joseph did not stop there, for in Ephraim's name, "fruitfulness," he pictured years ahead of increase for himself and his family.

During the seven years of famine, Joseph's brothers went down from Hebron to buy grain in Egypt. When Joseph saw them he remembered his dreams about the sheaves of grain, representing his brothers bowing down to him. When he revealed himself to his brothers, they were afraid—but Joseph comforted them and spoke kindly to them. Later, his father Jacob and all of his children and grandchildren came to live in the land of Goshen and be fed from the hand of Joseph—thus fulfilling his dreams.

When Jacob was coming to the end of his life, Joseph brought his two sons to his father to receive a blessing. But in blessing the boys Jacob did a very strange thing:

> Then Israel saw Joseph's sons, and said, "Who are these?" Joseph said to his father, "They are my sons, whom God has given me in this place." And he said, "Please bring them to me, and I will bless them." Now the eyes of Israel were dim with age, so that he could not see. Then Joseph brought them near him, and he kissed them and embraced them. And Israel said to Joseph, "I had not thought to see your face; but in fact, God has also shown me your offspring!" So Joseph brought them from beside his knees, and he bowed down with his face to the earth. And Joseph took them both, Ephraim with his right hand toward Israel's left hand, and Manasseh with his left hand toward Israel's right hand, and brought them near him. Then Israel stretched out his right hand and laid it on Ephraim's head, who was the younger, and his left hand on Manasseh's head, guiding his hands knowingly, for Manasseh was the firstborn. . . .
> Now when Joseph saw that his father laid his right hand on the head of Ephraim, it displeased him; so he took hold of his father's hand to remove it from Ephraim's head to Manasseh's head. And Joseph said to his father, "Not so, my father, for this one is the firstborn; put your right hand on his head." But his father refused and said, "I know, my son, I know. He also shall become a people, and he also shall be great; but truly his younger brother shall be greater than he, and his descendants shall become a multitude of nations." So he blessed them that

day, saying, "By you Israel will bless, saying, 'May God make you as Ephraim and as Manasseh!'" And thus he set Ephraim before Manasseh.

Genesis 48:8–14; 17–20

It was customary for the firstborn son to receive the right hand of blessing. Joseph thought that his father was making a mistake because of his blindness. But Jacob "guided his hands knowingly" and he crossed one arm over the other and put his right hand on the head of the youngest, who stood at his left, and his left hand on the head of the oldest, who stood at his right. Jacob knew by spiritual discernment that the younger would be the greater of the two. This was a work of divine preference and divine substitution. It was the same preference that God exhibited when He said to Jacob's mother, Rebekah, that Esau, the elder son, would serve his younger brother, Jacob.

This is the answer we have been seeking, the final clearing of the path. By setting Ephraim over Manasseh, Jacob was saying that Joseph's future fruitfulness would outweigh all the pain he endured in his past. That is the forgotten blessing!

Jesus

Now get ready, because we are about to see the reason that God initiated this blessing, this recourse for everyone who has known pain and desires to fill those hurt places with fruitfulness instead. I want to tell you of the last person in the Bible to wear a robe of many colors. His robe was also torn, but the tearing of His many-colored garment gives every Tamar and Joseph who has ever suffered the curse of rejection an open gateway to freedom, healing, restoration and fruitfulness. The prince who wore this many-colored robe removes all the pain that we have endured from words of iniquity. He even removes the memory of it. You might even say that the tearing of His many-colored coat is the doorway at the end of the path to the forgotten blessing.

The prince I am speaking about, of course, is Jesus—the Prince of Peace, the only begotten of the Father. Dear one, let these next words forever and always seal in your heart the fact that you are loved and cherished by your Father in heaven.

Where does Scripture teach that Jesus, the Prince of Peace, had a many-colored royal robe and that it was torn? We know that at the crucifixion Roman soldiers stripped Jesus of the robe He was wearing, but that robe was not torn. John records that:

> The soldiers, when they had crucified Jesus, took His garments and made four parts, to each soldier a part, and also the tunic. Now the tunic was without seam, woven from the top in one piece. They said therefore among themselves, "Let us not tear it, but cast lots for it, whose it shall be," that the Scripture might be fulfilled which says: "They divided My garments among them, and for My clothing they cast lots." Therefore the soldiers did these things.
>
> John 19:23–24

Jesus' robe was seamless, not torn, and from all accounts not a many-colored robe. So where is the royal, many-colored robe of Jesus? Let us take up the story in Matthew's gospel:

> And Jesus cried out again with a loud voice, and yielded up His spirit. Then, behold, the veil of the temple was torn in two from top to bottom; and the earth quaked, and the rocks were split.
>
> Matthew 27:50–51

The veil in the Temple served as a barrier, separating the people from the presence of God. Behind this heavy covering lay the room called the Holy of Holies, where the Ark of the Covenant and the mercy seat were kept. Once a year the high priest entered in beyond the veil and offered the blood of a sacrificial lamb as directed by God to make atonement for the sins of the people. The book of Exodus gives interesting information about this veil: It was many-colored. "You shall make a veil woven of blue, purple, and scarlet thread, and fine woven linen. It shall be woven with an artistic design of cherubim" (Exodus 26:31).

This many-colored covering was torn in two at the exact moment Jesus died. This symbolized the fact that the way was now open for all of us to enter into God's presence.

The book of Hebrews gives us further insight into the wonderful truth that lay behind the act in the Temple. It tells us that *the body of Jesus was the veil*:

> Therefore, brethren, having boldness to enter the Holiest by the blood of Jesus, by a new and living way which He consecrated for us, through the veil, that is, His flesh . . . let us draw near.
>
> Hebrews 10:19–20, 22

The tearing of Jesus' flesh literally opened the way for our healing and restoration with the Father.

As Jesus breathed His last breath, God the Father looked down through human history, and He saw every child who would face the effects of iniquity on the earth. God the Father saw every Joseph who would endure ridicule, rejection and physical abuse. His heart broke for every Tamar who would endure sexual abuse. His heart grieved for every woman who would endure the brutal blows of the sarcastic, destructive tongue of an unhealed husband. God looked down through the pages of future history and saw every person who would have his royal covering stripped away. And God tore His many-colored garment—the veil of the Temple—from top to bottom as a symbol that we might understand the work of redemption by Jesus on the cross.

Now think about our story of Jacob blessing Ephraim and Manasseh. Do you notice an unusual resemblance? When the many-colored veil was torn in two, God, by His sovereign choice and will, was exercising His divine preference—God crossed His hands!

You see, the same divine preference that God showed to Jacob over his elder brother, Esau, and to Ephraim over his older brother, Manasseh, was simply a foreshadowing of the preference He would show us over Jesus Christ, our elder brother!

God's only begotten Son was standing in front of His right hand, and you and I were standing in front of His left hand. But God crossed His hands, and placed the right hand of blessing over our heads, and His left hand on Jesus' head. We received the double-portion blessing, and Jesus received the curse of our sin. Jesus was our elder brother but, unlike Esau who fought to hold on to his birthright blessing, Jesus gave it to us out of love. Galatians 3:13–14 says:

> Christ has redeemed us from the curse of the law, having become a curse for us (for it is written, "Cursed is everyone who hangs on a tree"), that the blessing of Abraham might come upon the Gentiles in Christ Jesus, that we might receive the promise of the Spirit through faith.

Remember what God told Rebekah about her two sons? He told her that by divine preference the older would serve the younger. Jesus said in Matthew 20:28: "The Son of Man did not come to be served, but to serve, and to give His life a ransom for many." Our elder brother by an act of divine preference came to serve His younger siblings and give to us the birthright blessing. He was stripped, rejected and endured the tearing of His own body that we might enter into the presence of His Father and find restoration for our own rejection and pain.

The Scriptures teach in Isaiah 53:5 that Jesus was wounded for our transgressions and bruised for our iniquities. A wound is a puncture, cut or laceration on the outside skin of the body that causes bleeding. These cuts and wounds are obvious to us because they are visible. Transgressions are "outside" or external acts of sin. Thus, Jesus was wounded for our wounds; His lacerations were for our willful transgressions.

A bruise is caused by a traumatic impact of some kind and causes bleeding inside the body. The purple blotch that appears below the surface of the skin is evidence of internal bleeding. But internal bleeding is not always noticeable from the surface of the skin. Likewise, an internal bruise caused by the trauma of verbal abuse can exist undetected until it is dangerously out of control.

Just as Jesus was wounded for our wounds, He was bruised for our bruises—those blunt force traumas that caused us to bleed internally, either physically or emotionally. Dear one, only the blood of Jesus is sufficient to heal you of life's traumas. His internal hemorrhage is the only means to heal yours. Jesus was torn on the outside for our transgressions committed on the outside, and He was bruised on the inside for our iniquities working undercover on the inside.

This should remove all doubt concerning God's love for you and me! In fact, Jesus tells us that our Father in heaven plays no favorites. Yes, it is true: God the Father loves you every bit as much as He loves Jesus. Jesus said to His Father: "I in them, and You in Me; that they may be made perfect in one, and that the world may know that You have sent Me, and have loved them as You have loved Me" (John 17:23).

The next time you see a cross remember that God the Father crossed His hands and put His right hand of blessing on your head. Because God imparted to you and me the birthright blessing, we can lay aside the old, rotting garments passed down from another generation and begin our own stories—stories that will one day end in triumph, written by our loving Father.

Through the beautiful torn robe of your elder brother, Jesus, the passage is open. The thorns and snares are cleared away. In the Father's presence, you are covered and protected by His mercy. It is time now to learn how to live victoriously and walk in all of the blessings of Abraham. It is time now, through the substitutionary sacrifice of Jesus, to receive the forgotten blessing of Ephraim and Manasseh and forget all the pain of your father's house. It is time now to begin believing that your future fruitfulness will outweigh the pain of your past (see Ecclesiastes 7:8).

The passageway is clear. Let's move forward.

*** 7 ***

The Elements
of the Forgotten Blessing

Putting Your Words into Action

By faith Jacob, when he was dying, blessed each of the
sons of Joseph, and worshiped, leaning on the top of
his staff.

Hebrews 11:21

Have you ever been to a funeral? Generally at some point
in a funeral service comes a time for giving a eulogy. It
is a time of remembrance when the minister, relatives
and friends speak verbal blessings about the one who
has passed away. As we saw earlier, the word *blessing*
in Scripture is taken from the Greek word *eulogeo*. This
can be broken down into two parts: *eu* means "good"
and *logos* means "word." Put the two together and the

meaning of the word *blessing* is to speak a good word about another person.

I have always questioned why we wait until someone's funeral to give him his eulogy. Is there some unseen force that ties our tongues while the person is living and then lets go when he dies—freeing us finally to shower him with blessing? Interestingly, I have never heard an unkind word spoken about the dearly departed at a funeral. I once attended the funeral of a Chicago Mafia godfather. During the eulogy, even his enemies spoke of him as a blessed saint! He apparently lived life with the tender manners of the virgin Mary, Saint Peter and Mother Teresa combined!

At a funeral, everyone looks past the flaws and weaknesses of the departed and honors him or her with a good word. And rightly so. But wouldn't it be much more suitable—even logical—to eulogize someone when he or she is still breathing? Correct me if I am wrong, but I somehow believe that words of blessing will be of much greater benefit to the living than the dead!

But this rarely happens. It is much easier to look at the negative characteristics in others rather than the positive. That is why so often people belittle rather than eulogize others. Yet we are called upon to verbally bless those around us. To many, this is a foreign concept, but once you get into the habit of blessing you will never return to the sound of silence again. I am not calling you to "gushy" flattery but rather to sensible and strategic words of kindness.

In this chapter I want to give you practical principles for blessing others. Many people have taught about the different elements of the Lord's prayer and of the Aaronic blessing. I want to take a close look at the elements of the forgotten blessing that Jacob spoke over Ephraim and Manasseh. As we begin to bless others with the forgotten blessing, we will not only share a beautiful legacy of faith, but we ourselves, like Joseph, will be enriched with the Father's blessing. We appropriate, in a sense, the words that God spoke to Abraham: "In blessing I will bless thee" (Genesis 22:17, KJV). Since I have begun to bless my family and others outside of my immediate family with the forgotten blessing, my life has taken on rich, new meaning.

We are going to examine eight specific elements that Jacob incorporated in blessing his grandsons Ephraim and Manasseh:

1. The blessing was a natural part of Jewish life.
2. The blessing included a warm and loving embrace.
3. The blessing required the laying on of hands.
4. The person blessing shared his spiritual heritage.
5. The blessing included words of increase and expansion.
6. The person blessing required a degree of spiritual discernment.
7. The blessing was spoken.
8. The blessing required bold faith to bring results.

Let's look now at these eight key elements of the forgotten blessing.

1. It Is a Natural Part of Life

Then Israel saw Joseph's sons, and said, "Who are these?" Joseph said to his father, "They are my sons, whom God has given me in this place." And he said, "Please bring them to me, and I will bless them."

Genesis 48:8–9

Because of our pragmatic Western approach to life, we sometimes take something that is natural for another culture and make a formula out of it for ourselves. This is the case with the act of blessing. By adding too much planning and formality, we turn blessing into a one-time event—a formal, structured moment when we pronounce a blessing over someone. I highly encourage a more formal "night of blessing," but why not make verbal blessing a natural daily practice? If you study the lives of the patriarchs and biblical saints, you will see that their imparting of the blessing was anything but formal. Yes, they would often gather their children around their deathbeds and speak blessings to them, but this was at the end of a life in which it was the common practice to speak blessing consistently.

So first of all, make sure that speaking blessing is a natural part of your lifestyle. Don't wait until you are taking your last breath before you bless others! If you want to reap the rich benefits of reciprocal blessing, then make blessing a less formal and always natural outflow of your heart. Blessings can certainly be effective as part of a planned event, but few words are as sincere as a natural expression of blessing. So be spontaneous—Jacob was! Look at what he said: "Who are these kids with you, son?"

It is not that Jacob did not know his own grandsons. He was nearly blind. When Joseph informed him that the boys were his sons, Jacob responded immediately by saying, "Please bring them to me and I will bless them."

Speaking a blessing was as natural for Jacob as shaking hands is to us. One of my favorite stories about Jacob shows this to be true—the story of Jacob's audience with Pharaoh. I am sure that, prior to introducing his father to the king, Joseph coached Jacob in Egyptian etiquette and especially in how to address Pharaoh—a man the Egyptians believed to be a god. You would only speak when spoken to. You would kneel and bow and, by all means, never assume a raised position that was higher than Pharaoh's.

Do you suppose that old Jacob managed to hold the line on protocol in the presence of royalty? Of course not! Here is the account from Genesis 47:7–11:

> Then Joseph brought in his father Jacob and set him before Pharaoh; and Jacob blessed Pharaoh. Pharaoh said to Jacob, "How old are you?" And Jacob said to Pharaoh, "The days of the years of my pilgrimage are one hundred and thirty years; few and evil have been the days of the years of my life, and they have not attained to the days of the years of the life of my fathers in the days of their pilgrimage." So Jacob blessed Pharaoh, and went out from before Pharaoh.
>
> And Joseph situated his father and his brothers, and gave them a possession in the land of Egypt, in the best of the land, in the land of Rameses, as Pharaoh had commanded.

What actually happened in this story is quite incredible. Jacob the Jew is seated before the throne of the most powerful man in the world and, in the middle of their conversation, Jacob breaks all the formalities and says in essence: "Come down from your lofty throne, young man, because I want to speak a word of blessing over your life!"

Remember that the word *bless* means to "bend the knee." Jacob was seated before Pharaoh's throne so, for him to bless, Pharaoh had to come down to where Jacob was seated and bow before the man of God! I do not know what Jacob prayed, but I am sure it was beautiful! In fact, he spoke two different blessings, one when he came in and one when he went out.

Wouldn't you like to be known as a person of verbal blessing? I am not calling you to a lifestyle of extremes, but I am asking you to consider making verbal blessing a natural part of your lifestyle. Naturally I do not speak a word of blessing over everyone that I meet. I am, however, open to God's timing and at moments throughout my day He gives me unique opportunities to bless others verbally. I find that it is sometimes appropriate to pray a blessing over someone at the end of a phone conversation. Certainly I, as a pastor, bless those I have counseled with as we end our time together. The rule is, be sure it is natural and given at an appropriate time.

Many years after Jacob had died, another Pharaoh would ask for a blessing from a man of God. After the last plague that God brought upon Egypt, Pharaoh

> called for Moses and Aaron by night, and said, "Rise, go out from among my people, both you and the children of Israel. And go, serve the LORD as you have said. Also take your flocks and your herds, as you have said, and be gone; and bless me also."
>
> Exodus 12:31–32

I believe that during the four hundred years of the Israelites' enslavement to the Egyptians, they were known to bless the very ones that persecuted them. Because he knew that it was natural for Moses to bless, Pharaoh asked for his blessing as Moses departed.

I have tried to make the forgotten blessing a natural part of my lifestyle ever since I began to understand its common use in Jewish culture. My wife, Sharon, and I pray blessings over our children in the morning before they leave for school. We pray blessings in the evenings, before our family goes to bed. When friends of our teenagers visit, they often ask us to bless them before they leave. At the beginnning of every school year, when students are preparing to leave for college, they often come to our home and ask us to bless them. Verbally blessing others is becoming more and more natural to us!

2. It Includes a Warm and Loving Embrace

Now the eyes of Israel were dim with age, so that he could not see. Then Joseph brought them near him, and he kissed them and embraced them.

Genesis 48:10

Notice that, prior to the verbal blessing, Jacob gathered his grandsons close and embraced them. A warm embrace will often break down walls of resistance and send a message that words cannot express. A loving physical embrace is the partner to verbal blessing. Later, when Jacob blessed Manasseh and Ephraim, he laid his hands upon their heads. Thus, a warm embrace and the laying on of hands are two distinct and different elements of the forgotten blessing. It is recorded in Mark 10 that parents brought their children to Jesus that He might touch them: "And He took them up in His arms, laid His hands on them, and blessed them" (verse 16). Notice that there are three elements to the way Jesus blessed: an embrace, the laying on of hands and spoken words.

Some people try to maneuver around the element of embrace by saying, "I'm just not the type" or "It's not really my thing." But the warm embrace is an element of blessing that is biblical, natural and necessary. Remember the parable of the Prodigal Son? Jesus said that the first thing the prodigal's father did when the young man came to his senses and returned home was to embrace him. "And he arose and came to his father. But when he was still a great way off, his father saw him and had compassion, and ran and fell on his neck and kissed him" (Luke 15:20). The phrase *fell on his neck* speaks of a warm and tender embrace.

My home is filled with embracing. I have found that my verbal blessings will often fall on deaf ears if I have not first drawn in my family members with an affectionate touch. The father of the Prodigal Son took the first step toward restoring relationship with his son by running toward him and embracing him. It reminds me of the saying, "People don't care how much you know until they know how much you care." An embrace is a nonverbal expression of deep caring and concern, and it paves the way for verbal blessing. A warm embrace can break through the resistance of the hardest heart.

3. It Requires the Laying on of Hands

> Then Israel stretched out his right hand and laid it on Ephraim's head, who was the younger, and his left hand on Manasseh's head, guiding his hands knowingly, for Manasseh was the firstborn.
>
> Genesis 48:14

This is the first instance of the laying on of hands recorded in Scripture. Jacob used the laying on of hands to impart blessing, and from that moment forward the principle became a general biblical practice. Laying on of hands was used to ordain and commission ministry (see Exodus 29:1–28; Numbers 8:5–22; 27:18–22; Acts 6:1–6; 13:3; 1 Timothy 5:17–22); minister the baptism with the Holy Spirit (see Acts 9:17); pray for healing (see Mark 16:18); and impart spiritual gifts (see 2 Timothy 1:6). And as we noted earlier, Jesus imparted blessing with His hands (see Matthew 19:15; Luke 24:50).

The Hebrews believed that the laying on of hands imparted a responsibility and obligation to the one being blessed. The Hebrew word that describes the laying on of hands is *samak*, and it means to "press down upon" or "lean upon." The person receiving the blessing needed to be able to support the weight of the one imparting the blessing. Rabbis teach that there is much more to the laying on of hands than sticking your hands on someone's head. To them it is imparting the weight and responsibility required to carry out the words in the blessing.

I find it interesting that the "faith chapter" of Hebrews 11 gives us some insight into this principle of leaning on the one being blessed: "By faith Jacob, when he was dying, blessed each of the sons of Joseph, and worshiped, leaning on the top of his staff" (Hebrews 11:21). Jacob needed to lean upon his staff in order to stand. When he blessed Joseph's sons, with one hand on each of his grandsons' heads, the weight of his body would have been transferred to his hands. So we can see that Jacob must have leaned upon the heads of his grandsons as he blessed them. Perhaps it was this picture that became the foundation of the Hebrew understanding that with a blessing comes responsibility.

As you can see, the elements of affectionate embrace and the laying on of hands are two unique and distinct aspects of the forgotten blessing.

4. It Includes Sharing Your Spiritual Heritage

And he blessed Joseph, and said: "God, before whom my fathers Abraham and Isaac walked, the God who has fed me all my life long to this day, the Angel who has redeemed me from all evil, bless the lads."

Genesis 48:15–16

At this point Jacob had placed his hands on the heads of his grandsons and was giving a preamble to the verbal blessing he was about to speak. He wanted to make sure that his family knew about his relationship with God, and how his own personal faith had developed during his lifetime.

109

He started by saying that he was a third-generation believer: "God, before whom my fathers Abraham and Isaac walked." I think that Jacob wanted to be assured that Joseph and his sons knew that they were a part of a rich heritage of faith. Next he testified of God's provision: "the God who has fed me all my life long to this day." Finally he spoke of God's salvation: "the Angel who has redeemed me from all evil." Notice the progression in Jacob's spiritual odyssey: God of my fathers, God of my provision and God of my salvation. He began by saying that God was the God of his fathers, and ended by declaring that God has become his God as well.

It is very important that you share your spiritual odyssey with your family. Whether you are a first-generation believer or a third-generation believer, be sure to communicate where you have come from in your walk with Christ. Your personal testimony establishes your credibility in giving the blessing. In speaking the forgotten blessing you are imparting not only the Word of God, but part of yourself and character as well. Let people know where you have been.

My grandmother Rose communicated often her story of how, as a young Jewish woman, she saw a vision of Jesus. Her spiritual odyssey became a vital part of my own faith, and whenever she spoke words of blessing over me I felt connected to her rich heritage of faith and doctrine. Paul reminded Timothy of his spiritual journey when he said:

> I call to remembrance the genuine faith that is in you, which dwelt first in your grandmother Lois and your mother Eunice, and I am persuaded is in you also. Therefore I remind you to stir up the gift of God which is in you through the laying on of my hands.
>
> 2 Timothy 1:5–6

Paul not only reminds Timothy that he is a third-generation believer, but also that he has received an impartation from Paul himself. Paul never forgot his own spiritual journey, and he recited it often. *Share your testimony with others*—especially your family. When the enemy tries to break through the spiritual covering you are providing your family, it is your spiritual heritage —your testimony—that will help you prevail against him. Revelation 12:11 says, "And they overcame [the accuser of the brethren] by the blood of the Lamb and by the word of their testimony."

Now after Jacob had spoken of the God of his fathers, the God of his provision and the God of his salvation, he called on God to "bless the lads." Then he connected the children to their heritage by saying, "Let my name be named upon them, and the name of my fathers Abraham and Isaac" (Genesis 48:16). Jacob ended this element of the blessing by imparting to his grandsons the qualities of his entire spiritual lineage!

5. It Includes Words of Increase and Expansion

"And let them grow into a multitude in the midst of the earth."

Genesis 48:16

As you bless in faith, be specific in your projections. One thing I find throughout the many blessings recorded in the Scriptures is the principle of increase. In fact, a blessing would not be a blessing without the mention of expansion, fruitfulness and multiplication. Let's look at some of the blessings in the Scriptures.

- The blessing of man and woman: "And God blessed them, saying, 'Be fruitful and multiply'" (Genesis 1:22).

111

- The blessing of Noah: "And as for you, be fruitful and multiply; bring forth abundantly in the earth and multiply in it" (Genesis 9:7).

- The blessing of Abraham: "Blessing I will bless you, and multiplying I will multiply your descendants as the stars of the heaven and as the sand which is on the seashore" (Genesis 22:17).

- The blessing of Isaac: "And I will make your descendants multiply as the stars of heaven" (Genesis 26:4).

- Isaac's blessing of Jacob: "May God Almighty bless you, and make you fruitful and multiply you" (Genesis 28:3).

- Moses' blessing over Israel: "And He will love you and bless you and multiply you; He will also bless the fruit of your womb and the fruit of your land, your grain and your new wine and your oil, the increase of your cattle and the offspring of your flock" (Deuteronomy 7:13).

- David's blessing over Israel: "The LORD has been mindful of us; He will bless us; He will bless the house of Israel; He will bless the house of Aaron. He will bless those who fear the LORD, both small and great. May the LORD give you increase more and more, you and your children" (Psalm 115:12–14).

- Paul's blessing of the church in Thessalonica: "And may the Lord make you increase and abound in love to one another and to all, just as we do to you" (1 Thessalonians 3:12).

6. It Requires the Guidance of the Holy Spirit

Now when Joseph saw that his father laid his right hand on the head of Ephraim, it displeased him; so he took hold of his father's hand to remove it from Ephraim's head to Manasseh's head. And Joseph said to his father, "Not so, my father, for this one is the firstborn; put your right hand on his head." But his father refused and said, "I know, my son, I know. He also shall become a people, and he also shall be great; but truly his younger brother shall be greater than he, and his descendants shall become a multitude of nations."

Genesis 48:17–19

How did Jacob know that Ephraim would become greater than Manasseh? He simply saw something in Ephraim that he did not see in Manasseh. Perhaps Ephraim exhibited more leadership qualities than Manasseh. Perhaps Manasseh had a weakness in his character. This was not the first time Jacob had been around his grandsons. He had now lived in the land of Goshen for seventeen years (see Genesis 47:28), so there would have been many opportunities for him to examine the life and characteristics of Ephraim and Manasseh.

But keep in mind also that prior to the outpouring of the Spirit on the day of Pentecost, saints under the old covenant were led by the Spirit. This means that Jacob and the patriarchs had spiritual insight into the lives of those they blessed. Notice that as Jacob laid his hands on the young men he "guided his hands knowingly" (see verse 14). He had both spiritual discernment and practical knowledge of the boys' lives.

Thus, part of blessing another person is to tap into what God is already accomplishing within him or her and then to bless accordingly. God has blessed everyone with a certain spiritual gift or ability. It is usually easy to see where a person's God-given desires are, and the fruit that those desires produce.

113

But you also need to go a step further. If you are to be successful in giving a blessing, you must receive the mind of Christ and the direction of the Holy Spirit. Ask the Lord for His guidance. He will give you insight into the life of the one you are verbally blessing.

When Jacob blessed his own sons, some time later, we see again this combination of spiritual discernment and practical knowledge. Let's look at Jacob's blessing of his son Joseph:

"Joseph is a fruitful bough, a fruitful bough by a well; his branches run over the wall. The archers have bitterly grieved him, shot at him and hated him. But his bow remained in strength, and the arms of his hands were made strong by the hands of the Mighty God of Jacob (from there is the Shepherd, the Stone of Israel), by the God of your father who will help you, and by the Almighty who will bless you with blessings of heaven above, blessings of the deep that lies beneath, blessings of the breasts and of the womb. The blessings of your father have excelled the blessings of my ancestors, up to the utmost bound of the everlasting hills. They shall be on the head of Joseph, and on the crown of the head of him who was separate from his brothers."

Genesis 49:22–26

In the first half of the blessing, Jacob expressed his knowledge of Joseph's gifts and callings. In the second half, Jacob was led by the Spirit as he proclaimed details about Joseph's future. Always seek the Holy Spirit for direction and clarity before giving a blessing. Remember that a tongue that expresses blessing is a tree of life (see Proverbs 15:4), and that the words we speak will make the tree fruitful. Let's be certain that before we speak we know what kind of fruit God desires to produce.

7. It Requires Speaking

So he blessed them that day, saying, "By you Israel will bless, saying . . ."

Genesis 48:20

Keep in mind that we are talking about verbal blessing. For Jacob to communicate blessing, he needed to speak it. Osmosis and extrasensory perception are not alternatives to the spoken blessing! I am being humorous, of course, but at the same time I am conscious that we live in a silent culture. Sometimes it is tempting to take the pathway of least resistance—and even the *thought* of speaking a blessing can be frightening. I have seen men who are eloquent and verbally skilled melt like butter when it comes time to bless their children.

We have not walked down this ancient pathway before, so give yourself some time and patience to develop an aptitude for speaking blessing. When I first began to bless others, I wrote the blessings down ahead of time. At this point in my journey down the ancient path, speaking blessing comes more naturally, so I rarely write one down. On occasion, when I am speaking a blessing over a leader or one of my children, I will write it out so that we both have a record of what was said. Even so, these are cases when a *formal* blessing is being given. If you practice the principle, it will in time become more and more comfortable for you.

Examine the following Scriptures with me and see how blessing and speaking go together: "Jesus answered and said to him, 'Blessed are you, Simon Bar-Jonah'" (Matthew 16:17); "Then [Elizabeth] spoke out with a loud voice and said, 'Blessed are you among women'" (Luke 1:42); "And God blessed them, saying . . ." (Genesis 1:22).

115

8. It Requires Bold Faith

> By faith Jacob, when he was dying, blessed each of the sons of Joseph.
>
> Hebrews 11:21

Though our story of the forgotten blessing in Genesis 48 does not mention the word *faith*, it certainly implies it. Hebrews 11 makes it clear that the forgotten blessing will only be effective when spoken in faith: "By faith Jacob . . . blessed each of the sons of Joseph" (Hebrews 11:21). When you bless another person, you are proclaiming in faith what he or she shall become! The words you are speaking are not just empty sounds falling off of the tip of your tongue. By the power of a faith-filled spoken blessing you can speak life into another person's future. And when that person is in the coming generation, you also break the chains to your past.

Would you like a good place to start? Try blessing yourself with a faith-filled, spoken blessing! This is where Jacob began when he said to God, "I won't let you go unless You bless me." His asking—no, *demanding*—was bold, raw faith. Listen to the words of David and see if you detect any faith in this blessing with which he blessed himself:

> O God, who is like You? You, who have shown me great and severe troubles, shall revive me again, and bring me up again from the depths of the earth. You shall increase my greatness, and comfort me on every side.
>
> Psalm 71:19–21

If we take a closer look, we will see that the forgotten blessing in Genesis 48 is one of the most faith-filled blessings in Scripture. "So he blessed them that day, saying, 'By you Israel will bless, saying, "May God make you as Ephraim and as Manasseh!"'" (Genesis 48:20).

Jacob was literally saying, "From now on, whenever the Israelites bless, they will mention the names of Ephraim and Manasseh." It took bold faith to make that kind of projection, but there is something even of greater faith in Jacob's words.

Jacob, you see, was focusing on the meaning of his grandsons' names as well as remembering the pain and plight suffered in Joseph's life. When he said, "By you Israel will bless," he was speaking a word of faith—a word of abundance and freedom—over all of Israel! Is it any wonder that the Jewish people have not forgotten to pronounce Jacob's blessing?

Because we live in a culture of silence, it is quite possible that a person has passed from childhood into adulthood without ever receiving a spoken blessing. Because of this teaching on the forgotten blessing, I am sometimes called upon to speak at conferences on the subject. I find it fascinating that when I finish my message and ask if there are those present who would like to receive the spoken blessing of Ephraim and Manasseh most everyone responds.

At my first conference I was completely unprepared when more than five hundred people came forward to receive the blessing! People waited in line for over three hours to receive the simple words spoken by Jacob over his grandsons—a testament to the fact that our generation is desperate for verbal affirmation and words of blessing. Now I train the conference leaders to speak the blessing and together we can devote more time to each person.

After each conference I am overwhelmed by the comments in the letters and emails I receive from people aging from young adults to seniors. In general they tell me that they had been waiting their entire lives for those words of blessing. After receiving the spoken blessing and having the principles of the ancient pathway revealed to them, they were freed from the old wounds caused by verbal and emotional abuse and found themselves free to bless others out of the new reservoir of blessing flowing out of them.

You and I can also reap the wonderful benefits of this blessing if we will pronounce it in faith, because "those who are of faith are blessed with believing Abraham" (Galatians 3:9). By faith Jacob was proclaiming that you and I—later partakers of all of the blessings of Abraham through Christ—would be free from the pain of our pasts, and become fruitful in our future. According to Jacob's faith, our future will always be greater than our past.

These are the eight elements of the forgotten blessing. But how will you remember them the next time you have an opportunity to bless someone? Here is a simple outline that might help:

B: Bold faith
L: Laying on of hands
E: Embrace
S: Share your spiritual odyssey
S: Speak words of blessing
I: Increase is always part of the forgotten blessing
N: Natural blessings flow from a heart of faith
G: the Guidance of the Holy Spirit makes the
    difference

⊱ 8 ⊰

How to Bless Your Enemies

Breaking Your Chains

"You have heard that it was said, 'You shall love your neighbor and hate your enemy.' But I say to you, love your enemies, bless those who curse you, do good to those who hate you, and pray for those who spitefully use you and persecute you."

Matthew 5:43–44

Before World War II began, Adolph Eichman was a salesman who worked in his German homeland for an American oil company. But before the war was over he was personally responsible for the deaths of six million Jewish men, women and children. Eichman authored and oversaw the execution of Nazi Germany's "Final Solution"—the roadmap that called for the annihilation of European Jewry.

Eichman was captured and held in an American internment camp when Germany fell to the Allied forces. But with the help of the SS underground, he escaped, and for the next ten years he lived under an assumed name in Argentina with his family. In 1960 Israeli Mossad agents caught up with Eichman and covertly slipped him out of the country, drugged and clothed in an Israeli pilot's uniform. A special jail cell had been built for Eichman in the belly of an Israeli El Al commercial jetliner, and he was flown to Israel to stand trial. (A side note to this story: My cousin David Boxerman was avionics director of El Al at this time, and it was his assignment to design and build the jail cell. Another cousin, Colonel Samuel Wetzel, was the pilot of the jet that carried Eichman to justice.)

The trial of Adolph Eichman began on April 11, 1961, in Jerusalem. During the proceedings, an elderly victim of the concentration camps was called to testify about the atrocities he saw Eichman commit. The elderly man collapsed upon seeing Eichman, and was rushed to a hospital. He was interviewed after he had regained his composure, and asked the reason why he was overcome with such emotion at the sight of this murderous war criminal. Was it fear? Was it the awful memories that the presence of Eichman conjured up? Was it remorse for his loved ones who were tortured and killed?

The man's answer was startling. He was not overcome with fear when he saw the evil Eichman sitting in the courtroom. On the contrary, he was overcome because he had expected to see a murderous monster but instead laid his eyes upon a frightened old man. His shock was due to the fact that he realized Eichman is in all of us! He concluded that everyone of us has the potential for hatred and revenge.

Eichman was a common man who replayed and relived the hatred passed to him by others and, as a result, almost annihilated an entire race of people. He was responsible for his actions, but those actions were rooted in the way he allowed the hate of others to affect and change him. He made a choice.

Dear one, hateful things have happened to you—but you can choose whether or not those things become a part of you!

Let's face it: We live in a fallen world. Trans-generational, hate-filled verbal abuse has reached epidemic proportions. Jesus warned of this in Matthew 24:10 and 12 when He spoke about the climate of relationships during the last days: "And then many will be offended, will betray one another, and will hate one another. . . . And because lawlessness will abound, the love of many will grow cold." Notice that love gone cold, hatred and betrayal are all rooted in an offense. You can allow the trap of offense and unforgiveness to destroy you, or you can choose to forgive and bless the very ones who have harmed you.

In our journey down the ancient path of the forgotten blessing, we have cleared the thorns and thistles and can now see our way more clearly. That you are still reading and trudging on beyond the clearing process with me is a testament to your overwhelming desire to come to terms with your life and the conflicts you have endured. My hope and prayer is that at this point of our journey you have come to a place of releasing those who have offended you.

Dear one, we are not at the end of the ancient path yet. We are actually only at the beginning. We have only cleared the brush away—we have still to tread the path. The pathway to a life of blessing begins with forgiving your offenders and then blessing them. Yes, you heard me right! Blessing the very ones who have betrayed and cursed you. You probably know that forgiveness is a mark of our Christian life, but we will see in this chapter that verbally blessing an offender is a mandatory calling as

121

well. Forgiveness is oftentimes a matter of the heart, but blessing the one who initially brought the offense is the outward expression of a forgiving spirit.

Please hear me on this, because it is crucial to living a life that is receptive to God's blessing: *Verbally blessing your enemies opens the portal to victory over the curses spoken against you and breaks the chains to your past!*

In this chapter I am going to teach you how to bless those who persecute you. Are you ready for the ride of your life? When I first experienced the exhilarating freedom that blessing an offender imparted, I felt as if I were a child again, riding the Big Dipper Roller Coaster at the Santa Cruz Beach and Boardwalk.

There is an initial fear to blessing an enemy, just as there was to riding the Big Dipper as a child. I can remember buying the fifty-cent ticket and waiting by myself in the thirty-minute line because all of my friends were too afraid to go. The Big Dipper was one of the only remaining wooden roller coasters on either coast, and the wooden frame groaned eerily at every twist and turn of the brightly colored cars.

Unlike the roller coasters of today, the Big Dipper's boarding platform was located toward the top of the track, so the brave-hearted passengers first had to climb stairs to that frightening height. The stairway was narrow and winding and filled with the scents of cotton candy, tanning oil, salt water taffy, hair wax and new rubber sneakers. I admit that my first trip up the "stairway of death" was so frightening that when I reached the top I turned around, embraced the humiliation and walked all the way down to freedom and safety—past about a hundred half-smiles of mixed empathy and pity. That particular spring day was the opening day of the new season, and the first time my height had matched the legal measuring line for Dipper passengers. After waiting every summer of my entire life to prove my fearlessness, the trek downward seemed to take another lifetime.

I remember reaching the street level and looking upward to see the Dipper climb noisily to the summit and then plunge downward toward the crashing waves of the Pacific Ocean. The red, blue, purple and green cars were filled with screaming children raising their hands to the heavens. That I should stand in safety while others enjoyed the ride of their lives was to me no freedom at all!

I decided that I might die on the Dipper, but that I could not live with myself unless I reached the summit. I looked at the ticket I held in my hand, closed my eyes and walked back to rejoin the long line. It was my first flight into freedom.

Choosing to bless an enemy is something like climbing the stairs to board the Big Dipper. Yes, you can live in obedience and relative freedom by forgiving in your heart the one who uncovered and harmed you. But until you speak blessing, you will remain on the street level, always looking up at the others who have taken the exhilarating plunge from the summit.

Please, take the ticket and climb the stairway to blessing your enemies. It may take you a few tries and, like me, you may run back down the stairs in fear, but before long you will be rickety-racketing your way to the summit with uplifted hands, ready for the rush of victory. Are you ready for the ride of your life? All aboard! Let's first look at six benefits of blessing those who have cursed you.

Benefit 1: Completeness

Blessing the one who has cursed you will make you a "complete" Christian. Listen to the words of Christ in the Sermon on the Mount:

"You have heard that it was said, 'You shall love your neighbor and hate your enemy.' But I say to you, love your enemies, bless those who curse you, do good to those who hate you, and pray for those who spitefully use you and persecute you, that you may be sons of your Father in heaven; for He makes His sun rise on the evil and on the good, and sends rain on the just and on the unjust. For if you love those who love you, what reward have you? Do not even the tax collectors do the same? And if you greet your brethren only, what do you do more than others? Do not even the tax collectors do so? Therefore you shall be perfect, just as your Father in heaven is perfect."

Matthew 5:43–48

Jesus was not merely commanding us to bless the people we have personality conflicts with. He was talking about people who hate you, despise you and verbally curse and persecute you! He was talking about the person who willfully betrays you and uses you for his or her own ends. He was talking about the person who deceives you and steals your goods. Jesus says that if we will verbally bless such a person we will be "perfect." This little word, *perfect*, is the Greek word *teleios*, and it means "whole, complete and mature." Verbally blessing an offender brings us into the blessing of wholeness and maturity! Remember the word of the Lord to Abraham: "In blessing I will bless you." Jesus is not making a suggestion here, but rather giving us a command—to bless those who curse us. He knows that we will never be complete and whole without taking this difficult plunge.

Benefit 2: Release

Blessing the one who has cursed you releases you from many of life's pressures. Let's look again at Christ's Sermon on the Mount:

"You have heard that it was said, 'An eye for an eye and a tooth for a tooth.' But I tell you not to resist an evil person. But whoever slaps you on your right cheek, turn the other to him also. If anyone wants to sue you and take away your tunic, let him have your cloak also. And whoever compels you to go one mile, go with him two."

Matthew 5:38–41

Jesus commands us: "I tell you not to resist an evil person." The word *resist* in this passage is the Greek word *anthistemi*, and it means to oppose vigorously. It carries the connotation of standing one's ground in face-to-face confrontation. Jesus says not to do this. Interestingly, *anthistemi* is the Greek root word of our English *antihistamine*. We take antihistamines to fight symptoms of colds and allergic reactions. Jesus is telling us here to quit resisting and confronting the person who has set out to slander and betray us. We live in a culture of contention that says: "Don't yield to anyone! Fight for your rights! Defend yourself at all costs!" But along comes Jesus commanding us to get out of the fight and to bless the person who wants to take advantage of us by giving him our right and left cheeks, our tunics and our committed service! He is calling us to trust in God to vindicate and cover us. When we are willing to do this, there is an awesome release from life's burdens and pressures.

Benefit 3: Changed Hearts

Blessing your enemy will produce in him a spirit of repentance. Paul said in Romans 12:17–21:

Repay no one evil for evil. Have regard for good things in the sight of all men. If it is possible, as much as depends on you, live peaceably with all men. Beloved, do

125

not avenge yourselves, but rather give place to wrath; for it is written, "Vengeance is Mine, I will repay," says the Lord. Therefore "If your enemy is hungry, feed him; if he is thirsty, give him a drink; for in so doing you will heap coals of fire on his head." Do not be overcome by evil, but overcome evil with good.

There are several interpretations of what Paul meant by "heap[ing] coals of fire" on an enemy's head, but most agree that the context is repentance. When we bless an evil person with good, our righteous actions will ultimately usher in conviction and bring the person to repentance.

Benefit 4: Protection

Blessing your enemy preserves and protects your life. When we refuse to bless our enemies and curse them instead, we grieve the Holy Spirit and open ourselves up to God's judgment. Notice these words in Paul's letter to the Ephesian Christians:

Let no corrupt word proceed out of your mouth, but what is good for necessary edification, that it may impart grace to the hearers. And do not grieve the Holy Spirit of God, by whom you were sealed for the day of redemption. Let all bitterness, wrath, anger, clamor, and evil speaking be put away from you, with all malice.

Ephesians 4:29–31

It is clear from this and other passages of Scripture that when we feel the need to defend ourselves with retaliatory words of cursing, we quench and grieve the Holy Spirit. It may sound self-centered but it is very biblical to preserve your life through the peacefulness of your tongue. Job said:

I have [not] rejoiced at the destruction of him who hated me, or lifted myself up when evil found him (indeed I have not allowed my mouth to sin by asking for a curse on his soul).

Job 31:29–30

Job is saying here that cursing an enemy is a sin before God. We remove ourselves from God's protective covering when we succumb to cursing an enemy.

Benefit 5: Freedom

Blessing your enemy is your gateway to freedom! The children of Israel served as slaves to Pharaoh for four hundred years. Because Egypt would not allow God's people to leave and journey to the land of promise, God sent a series of plagues upon the land to compel Pharaoh to let the people go. We read this verse earlier, but notice its import: The last act of Moses on his way out of Egypt was to bless the man who had enslaved his family. There were many supernatural factors involved in the exodus of the Jews, but I find it astonishing that the key that finally opened the portal to promise was a verbal blessing:

Then [Pharaoh] called for Moses and Aaron by night, and said, "Rise, go out from among my people, both you and the children of Israel. And go, serve the LORD as you have said. Also take your flocks and your herds, as you have said, and be gone; and bless me also."

Exodus 12:31–32

Though Scripture does not record the actual event, I am sure that Moses complied and placed his hands upon Pharaoh and blessed him with a wonderful blessing. Was it the blessing of Ephraim and Manasseh? Perhaps so.

That Pharaoh would ask for a blessing tells me that it was a common thing for the Jews to verbally bless the one who was enslaving them.

Benefit 6: Blessings

Blessing your enemy is the key that unlocks the double-portion blessing.

In our study we have examined the life and character of Joseph. It would have been easy for him to allow thoughts of unforgiveness and revenge to rule his spirit after enduring the pain that his brothers brought upon him. But upon revealing himself to his brothers, Joseph said, "But now, do not therefore be grieved or angry with yourselves because you sold me here; for God sent me before you to preserve life" (Genesis 45:5). Not only did Joseph bless them verbally, he went one step further and encouraged his brothers to forgive themselves of any lasting guilt for what they had done to him! Later on, when his brothers feared that Joseph might take revenge upon them, they fell down before him and declared that they were his servants. Joseph told them:

> "Do not be afraid, for am I in the place of God? But as for you, you meant evil against me; but God meant it for good, in order to bring it about as it is this day, to save many people alive. Now therefore, do not be afraid; I will provide for you and your little ones." And he comforted them and spoke kindly to them.
>
> Genesis 50:19–21

Was Joseph rewarded for not paying back evil for evil? Yes! Though Joseph was not the firstborn son, he received the birthright blessing of the double portion. After Jacob finished blessing his two grandsons Ephraim

128

and Manasseh, he blessed Joseph with these words: "Moreover I have given to you one portion above your brothers, which I took from the hand of the Amorite with my sword and my bow" (Genesis 48:22). Maintaining a forgiving spirit in the face of evil and then expressing the spirit of forgiveness through verbal blessing will always unlock for you a double portion of blessing from your Father in heaven.

It is true that blessing someone who has harmed you might be the most difficult thing you have ever done. You might feel resistant at first, but I can assure you that verbal blessing is the key to unlocking many unopened doors in your future. After you take your first flight over the summit and begin enjoying the blessing that obedience brings, there will be many more trips up to the boarding platform to bless your enemies. Let's now look at four ways you can do this.

1. Speak Well of Your Enemies

Jesus said, "Bless those who curse you" (Luke 6:28). Remember that the word *bless* from the Greek language is taken from the words *eu*, which means "well," and *logos*, which means "speech." Put the two words together, and you have *eulogy* or *eulogize*. The word *eulogy* basically means "to speak well of." When we bless an enemy we are, in essence, speaking well about her to others and to her as well. Keep in mind that the principle of blessing is not accomplished in the mind but rather with the tongue. It is verbal. The word means *speaking well*, not just *thinking well*! If you just think about forgiveness rather than expressing the spirit of forgiveness through the act of eulogizing your enemy, you will forever be on the street level watching others cascading over the summit into the double-portion blessing God has prepared for them. Without verbally blessing the one who has abused you and taken advantage of you, you will never grasp completeness and wholeness in Christ.

2. Pray for Your Enemies

Not only are we to bless the ones who have cursed us, we are also called to pray for them. Jesus said in Luke 6:28: "Pray for those who spitefully use you." Listen to the words of David as he describes a prayer that he prayed for an enemy who had become ill:

> Fierce witnesses rise up; they ask me things that I do not know. They reward me evil for good, to the sorrow of my soul. But as for me, when they were sick, my clothing was sackcloth; I humbled myself with fasting; and my prayer would return to my own heart. I paced about as though he were my friend or brother; I bowed down heavily, as one who mourns for his mother.
>
> Psalm 35:11–14

Jesus prayed for the hate-filled mob who stood beneath His cross, "Father, forgive them, for they do not know what they do" (Luke 23:34). Steven prayed for the very ones who were stoning him to death: "Then he knelt down and cried out with a loud voice, 'Lord, do not charge them with this sin'" (Acts 7:60).

Here is a prayer of blessing for an enemy that I think might help you:

"Lord, today I bring to you in prayer the person who has done one or more of the following to me:

- Verbally cursed and abused me
- Betrayed me

130

- Despitefully used me
- Falsely accused me
- Stolen my goods
- Physically or sexually abused me

"First of all, Lord, I forgive and release this person from any feelings of revenge, hatred or anger within me. Now I bless this person, and I ask You to bless him [or her].

- Bless his life with riches and honor
- Bless his home with kindness, joy and love
- Bless him with healing and wholeness
- Bless him with integrity and wisdom
- Bless the good works of his hands
- Bless his mind, will and emotions with the peace of God
- Bless him with the desire to follow the leading of the Holy Spirit

"I pray, Lord, that You will bless him with the blessing of Ephraim and Manasseh and that he would forget the pain of his past and be fruitful in his future. I pray that You will bless him and keep him, and cause Your face to shine upon him and be gracious to him and give him peace. I pray that Your strong name will be upon him. Amen."

3. Prepare a Meal for Your Enemies

Romans 12:20 says: "If your enemy is hungry, feed him; if he is thirsty, give him a drink." I know that this sounds farfetched, but it is a biblical principle that deserves our attention: We are to help supply the needs of our enemies in practical ways. One of the greatest conquerors in history was Cyrus the Great. When nations fell before him, it was his practice immediately to comfort his enemies and feed them, many times allowing them to remain in power under his new governorship. In so doing he showed mercy to his enemies and guaranteed that future uprisings against his sovereign rule would be few.

The prophet Elisha fed the enemies of Israel, and it became the key that established long lasting peace between Israel and Syria:

> Now when the king of Israel saw [the captive Syrian army], he said to Elisha, "My father, shall I kill them? Shall I kill them?" But he answered, "You shall not kill them. Would you kill those whom you have taken captive with your sword and your bow? Set food and water before them, that they may eat and drink and go to their master." Then he prepared a great feast for them; and after they ate and drank, he sent them away and they went to their master. So the bands of Syrian raiders came no more into the land of Israel.
>
> 2 Kings 6:21–23

4. Show Kindness and Mercy to Your Enemies

Can you trust God to cover and protect you as you bless your offenders? That is really what it is all about, isn't it? Trust. When it comes down to it, you and I have many fears about speaking well of our enemies because we don't trust God to cover and protect us. Beyond that, our greatest fear is the same fear that captivated Jonah.

God told Jonah to take a message of repentance and judgment to the Ninevites. The Ninevites were hated, heathen enemies of the Jews, and Jonah wanted nothing to do with them. Jonah ran from the call to bless his enemies because he was afraid that God just might show them mercy. He repented only after his running away from the protective covering of God landed him in a whale of a problem. Jonah finally preached the Word of the Lord to the Ninevites and, amazingly, they repented and God showed them mercy.

Here is the record of Jonah's anger toward God when He had mercy on Jonah's enemies:

> Then God saw their works, that they turned from their evil way; and God relented from the disaster that He had said He would bring upon them, and He did not do it. But it displeased Jonah exceedingly, and he became angry. So he prayed to the LORD, and said, "Ah, LORD, was not this what I said when I was still in my country? Therefore I fled previously to Tarshish; for I know that You are a gracious and merciful God, slow to anger and abundant in lovingkindness, One who relents from doing harm."
>
> Jonah 3:10–4:2

Later God would say to Jonah: "And should I not pity Nineveh, that great city, in which are more than one hundred and twenty thousand persons who cannot discern between their right hand and their left?" (Jonah 4:11).

You see, God wants everyone to be saved and to come to the knowledge of the truth of His Son. The very ones who have harmed and hurt you are on God's heart! He loves them and sent His Son to die for them. Your act of mercy and kindness toward them may be the very thing that opens their hearts to Christ and brings them to a place of receiving God's blessing. Yes, it is true: Our merciful, loving God desires the best for our enemies. When the enemies of Christ came to arrest Him, it was His mercy that reattached the ear of the high priest's servant after Peter had cut it off with a sword. God wills to show mercy even to evil people. Look at the words of Christ in Luke 6:35–36:

> "But love your enemies, do good, and lend, hoping for nothing in return; and your reward will be great, and you will be sons of the Most High. For He is kind to the unthankful and evil. Therefore be merciful, just as your Father also is merciful."

This is often the main reason why we *don't* bless our enemies—we are afraid that God might just show them mercy and answer our words of blessing! I know that you might have to swallow hard to accept this, but it is true nonetheless. I am afraid that too many of us are running from the call to bless our enemies and boarding a ship with Jonah, headed in the opposite direction. Deep down we do not *want* our enemies to be blessed—and we would rather live on the street level, riding the kiddy whale ride, than cascade into freedom at the cost of blessing our enemies.

What it really comes down to is faith—faith in God's promise that He will reward you for blessing an offender, faith in His promise that in blessing others He will bless you. David had faith in God's provision and proclaimed in his now-famous 23rd Psalm, "You prepare a table before me in the presence of my enemies" (Psalm 23:5).

It is true that we live in a fallen world that produces fallen evil people like Adolph Eichman. It may even have been a monster like Eichman who tried to destroy your life. But hate and revenge toward your offender will produce only the bitter residue of Eichman in you. Someone once said that revenge is the sweetest morsel ever cooked in hell. I believe they were right. Revenge tastes sweet initially, but its side effects shatter the human spirit. You will find that blessing an enemy causes a river of satisfaction and comfort to flow your way and frees you to live in completeness and wholeness. There are many stories I can tell you about the healing that flows toward a person who blesses the one who has cursed him but the following is my favorite. The story I am about to tell you is true. It is an all-too-common story told to me by countless people I meet in airplanes and coffee shops. It is such a common story these days that people share it in a matter-of-fact manner as if they have grown used to it. The ending to this story is, however, anything but common.

Jim was a young executive living and working in the Chicago Loop, and he faithfully attended the church I pastored in the downtown area. I had known Jim for about two years when he came to see me one day and shared several life issues that he could not seem to overcome. My first question to him was: "Jim, tell me about the relationship you have with your father." Jim shared with me that when he was five years old his father had deserted him and his four siblings, never to return. No one had heard from him in 25 years. Jim's dad had made a few enemies with Chicago's crime family. His mother suspected that he had been placed on their hit list and fled to preserve his life.

Through several discussions of Jim's issues we determined that much of the baggage Jim was carrying around had to do with the shame and guilt of abandonment by his father and the resulting anger and pain that had been buried most of his life. I encouraged Jim to begin taking steps to locate his father and bring resolution to this painful ordeal. This proposal seemed unreasonable to Jim and he was angry about the idea of forgiving his father for rejecting him. The stairway to the boarding platform of the Big Dipper was too steep.

After several weeks of talking with me about the power of forgiveness and blessing those who curse you, Jim agreed to write his father a letter of blessing. Even though

Jim's family had no idea where the father lived, or even if he was alive, I told him that writing the letter would break the chains of the curse and bring freedom to his life. In the letter Jim assured his father that his forgiveness was genuine and he concluded the letter with a blessing. When he was finished he signed it, sealed it and placed it in his desk drawer. What happened next is a wonderful example of the power of blessing your enemies.

When Jim closed his desk drawer he also closed the chapter to 25 years of family estrangement and unresolved issues. At that very moment the phone on his desk rang and when he put the receiver to his ear he heard these words: "Jim, this is your father." Over the previous several weeks, Jim's father had come to a place of longing to reconnect with his children. He was terminally ill, and wanted to resolve things before he died. He had somehow located his eldest daughter's phone number, and she had given him the telephone numbers of the rest of his children. He was living in another state and wanted to meet with his son!

A few weeks later I was invited to lunch with Jim and his dad in a downtown Chicago restaurant. This luncheon was their first meeting in 25 years, and there was understandably a little tension at first. Soon, however, we all came to realize that Jim's sense of humor was much like his father's, and I sat spellbound as the two of them shared about their lives. Talk about a wild ride on the Dipper! This was for Jim the ride of his life, and I had the privilege of seeing Jim and his father go over the top together—hands up in the air—grinning all the way! Jim's father passed away within a few months. Through Jim's willingness to bless the one who abandoned and uncovered him, he opened the door to resolution and healing.

By walking in forgiveness, you are finding sure footing on the ancient pathway of blessing. By blessing your offenders, you are choosing to set aside bitterness and hatred in order to receive the double-portion blessing. A glorious life absent of relational pressures and filled with fruitfulness and completeness awaits you.

Our next step in the journey hits close to home. It is one that literally saved my relationship with my family. Keep reading to find out how to bless your family members.

✤ 9 ✤

How to Bless Your Household

Making the Most of Your Opportunity

Then David returned to bless his household.

2 Samuel 6:20

King David was not doing anything out of the ordinary in blessing his household. Following Jewish custom, David no doubt gathered his family around him after the evening meal and blessed them verbally. He laid his hands upon the heads of his children and most probably prayed the customary blessing: "May you be like Ephraim and Manasseh." In other words, "May you forget the pain of your past and may you be fruitful in your future."

When I first discovered this ancient path a few years ago, I began feeling a deep remorse for the missed opportunities I had had to bless my family. But then I read a Scripture that changed my perspective. In our study of Joseph we discovered how, as a young teenage boy,

139

he was verbally abused and rejected by his brothers and sold as a slave. I can only imagine the remorse his father felt when Joseph was later united with his family, knowing that so many years had been lost between them. But God in His mercy restored those years between father and son. Jewish tradition tells us that Joseph was seventeen years old when he was separated from his father. Scripture tells us that when he was reunited with his father, the two of them enjoyed seventeen years together before Jacob's death: "And Jacob lived in the land of Egypt seventeen years. So the length of Jacob's life was one hundred and forty-seven years" (Genesis 47:28).

I believe that age-long family issues and conflicts were resolved during this period of time, and Jacob had the opportunity to bless not only his son Joseph, but his grandsons Ephraim and Manasseh as well. Jacob's most productive spoken blessings were pronounced over his family in his old age. Dear saint, do not live with any regrets from your past. God will graciously restore the lost years to you! You are now walking on the path of the forgotten blessing and, because of your willingness to forget the pain of your past and bless the very ones who have cursed you, your future will be filled with fruitfulness and completeness. Your future will be greater than your past.

In this chapter we are going to discover how to bless our households. Now that we have found this ancient pathway, we have a wonderful opportunity to bless the coming generation. My prayer is that the principles of the forgotten blessing will not only help you to resolve the pain from your past but will be a significant life-principle that you impart to your children and grandchildren! Again, remember that "a wholesome tongue is a tree of life" (Proverbs 15:4). It is the wholesome tongue of blessing that causes the next generation to produce good fruit. Your tongue determines the health of your seed. Are you ready to release the forgotten blessing in your household and then watch how it restores, heals and nourishes your family? Here we go!

George Barna is a Christian pollster. He polls the church in America on issues like morality, theology, politics and economics. Barna recently published a book about Christian parenting that is a landmark work for our generation of parents. It is called *Transforming Children into Spiritual Champions*.

Barna's premise is simple: Christian parents in general have abdicated their responsibility for imparting biblical principles to their children, and are completely dependent upon religious professionals at the local church level to fulfill this task. It is good for children to learn in the church environment, but the best place to instruct a child has always been the home. Church ministries should be there only to enhance and confirm what mothers and fathers are teaching. The findings of the Barna Research Group are shocking. Here are some of Barna's conclusions:

> Our national surveys have shown that while more than 4 out of 5 parents (85 percent) believe they have the primary responsibility for the moral and spiritual development of their children, more than two out of three of them abdicate that responsibility to their church. Their virtual abandonment of leading their children spiritually is evident in how infrequently they engage in faith-oriented activities with their young ones. For instance, we discovered that in a typical week, fewer than 10 percent of parents who regularly attend church with their kids read the Bible together, pray together (other than at meal times) or participate in an act of service as a family unit. Even fewer families—1 out of every 20—have any type of worship experience together with their kids, other than while they are at church during a typical month.

141

In short, most families do not have a genuine spiritual life together. However, we also found that this is not disturbing to most of them for two reasons. First, they are merely following the precedent that was set for them. In other words, American parents—even those who are born-again churchgoers described by their church as "pillars"—are generally doing what their parents did with them: dropping off the kiddies at church and allowing the religious professionals to mastermind the spiritual development of the young people. No matter how much church leaders preach about the need for parents to personally invest in the spiritual growth of children, adults tend to revert to what was modeled for them, noting that carting the kids to church and occasional religious events is sufficient. "After all," explained one mother, echoing a sentiment that has become a very common reply emerging from our research, "that's what my parents did with me and I turned out pretty good." This notion of turning out "pretty good" is especially widespread among Baby Boomers.

Second, most churchgoing parents are neither spiritually mature nor spiritually inclined and, therefore, they do not have a sense of urgency or necessity about raising their kids to be spiritual champions.[13]

It is evident that we have a problem. Now what can we do to solve it and begin a pattern of family life that communicates God's works and wonders from generation to generation? Here are six practical things you can do to bless your household:

1. Plan a Special Family Blessing Night

Verbal blessing should be a daily habit for all of us, but planning a special weekly time of blessing will imprint a wonderful memory upon your family's heart. It is sad that spiritually directed family gatherings are few and far between. I encourage you to set aside one night every week when you can spend a few hours together as a family. You might want to begin with a family mealtime.

By all means instruct everyone present to turn off cell phones, landline phones, pagers, computers, televisions and radios! This might generate resistance at first, but it is impossible to communicate with each other when MTV or a news network is vying for your attention. I can only imagine what would have happened between Jesus and His disciples at the Last Supper if cell phones were in vogue.

Jesus: "But I say to you, I will not drink of this fruit of the vine from now on until—"

Beep-boop-boop-beep-bah-beep!

John: [Reaches into his satchel and fumbles around for his cell phone. He looks at the display, thinks for a moment before speaking.] "Sorry, Master, but I need to take this call. It's the Sea of Galilee Fish Market, and I think they've got a buyer for James' boat!"

Every mind at the table (except Jesus', of course) would have been taken back to the windswept shores of Galilee, their past lives and the going cost of medium-size fishing boats. Jesus would have had to perform a miracle just to get through the supper without interruption!

Now, until I learned the power of verbal blessing, our family devotional times were a bore. There was little family participation and the sound of my voice droning on through the evening put everyone (including my wife) to sleep. I am afraid that my kids dreaded family night! But here is what we do now: After supper together we gather in our family room and share prayer needs. The needs range from finding the right college to sick pets. (We have even held funeral services for goldfish during our family prayer time: "And now, Lord, may Speedy enter into your eternal rest. . . .")

Each person shares a need, and the person sitting to his or her right prays about that person's request. After our time of prayer, we read a passage of Scripture and discuss its meaning and application to our family. Next, we enter into a time of blessing. Each person in our family receives a verbal blessing from the other family members. When a person's time comes to be blessed, the others share a good word about him or her. The blessing might be about an aspect of the person's calling, gifting or personality. We have six people in our immediate family, so we each receive five verbal blessings every family night!

Sharon and I lay hands on the heads of each of our children individually and bless them with the forgotten blessing: "May you be like Ephraim and Manasseh—may you forget the pain of your past and may you bear much fruit in your future." During this time of individually blessing our children, Sharon and I use the elements of the blessing discussed in chapter 8, speaking specific blessings over each child. Through our careful, everyday examining of our children's gifts and talents, we are well prepared to bless the natural and spiritual gifts that each one has. We try not to respond to any negative behavior on our children's part but rather bless them for what they shall one day become. When Isaac blessed his two sons, he was blessing them according to the characteristics he saw in them and how these giftings would develop in the future: "By faith Isaac blessed Jacob and Esau concerning things to come" (Hebrews 11:20). Here is an example of how we point out to our children the special gifts and callings we observe in them:

Rachel: artistic; issue-oriented; single-minded; inspiring qualities of leadership; a strong will that is under the influence of the Holy Sprit; compassionate toward hurting and underprivileged people; a heart for evangelism and missions; affectionate; loving; just.

Elizabeth: energetic; a wistful personality; carefree yet disciplined; organized; a soul-winner; a strong evangelistic gifting and anointing; the gift of helps; networker; discerner of the times; thinks and plans ahead; submitted heart; truthful; humble; loves a challenge.

Hannah: prophetic gifting; gift of discernment; insightful; holy; sweet spirit; compassionate; witty; friend that sticks closer than a brother; teacher; detailed; unencumbered; unburdened; special; intercessor.

Nathan: determined; devoted; eagle who stays close to the nest; consistent; kind and gentle spirit in whom there is nothing false; one who will be committed to others in lifelong relationships; one who does not waiver.

After this, my four children and I bless Sharon according to Proverbs 31:28–31:

> Her children rise up and call her blessed; her husband also, and he praises her: "Many daughters have done well, but you excel them all." Charm is deceitful and beauty is passing, but a woman who fears the LORD, she shall be praised. Give her of the fruit of her hands, and let her own works praise her in the gates.

Sharon then lays hands upon my head, and she and our children bless me with the words of Psalm 128:

> Blessed is every one who fears the LORD, who walks in His ways. When you eat the labor of your hands, you shall be happy, and it shall be well with you. Your wife shall be like a fruitful vine in the very heart of your house, your children like olive plants all around your table. Behold, thus shall the man be blessed who fears the LORD. The LORD bless you out of Zion, and may you see the good of Jerusalem all the days of your life. Yes, may you see your children's children. Peace be upon Israel!

2. Bless Your Romance

It is important that children know that their parents not only love them, but also love each other. Proverbs 5:18 says: "Let your fountain be blessed, and rejoice with the wife of your youth." In our family time, I often not only bless Sharon according to Proverbs 31 but will also bless our marriage, that it may continue to bear the fruits of long-lasting joy and happiness. Here is an example of a blessing over the romance of marriage. A husband and wife should read this in the presence of their children:

"We bless the fountain of love in our home. We bless our words that they will always remain soft and tender. We bless our right hands that we have pledged in covenant relationship that our bond will always remain strong. We bless our eyes that we will delight only in one another. We bless our hearts that they will always be full of passion. We bless our conversations that they will never be given to boredom or sameness. We bless our bodies that we will remain healthy and live a long, satisfied and fulfilled life together. We bless our memories that they will only be sweet. We bless our lips that each and every kiss will feel like the first one. We bless our children with the ability to choose mates who express the fruits of the Holy Spirit. We bless our children's future marriage relationships with health, longevity and love."

3. Bless Your Substance

You as a family are stewards over the things God has given you. During our family gathering we take time to bless the things that are under our care: our finances, our material things such as cars and computers, and our home. This is scriptural, and the practice will help your children to realize the value of taking care of the things that God has blessed them with. You may think that it is strange to bless inanimate objects, but I have certainly seen people curse them! I have always been amused at how quick we are to curse a broken copy machine or malfunctioning computer—but how slow we are to bless it!

We have all seen a motorist on the side of the road, standing next to a disabled vehicle, kicking the tires and cursing the car. We curse the aches and pains in our bodies, the economy, our jobs and our finances. We even curse good ol' George Washington when we say things like, "A dollar sure doesn't go as far as it used to." I have a friend who broke his big toe while kicking and cursing his lawnmower for failing to start.

If you desire for the things under your stewardship to last for a long time, then certainly change the oil when necessary, water the lawn and paint the shutters. But also speak words of blessing over them. Jesus conferred a benefit of blessing over one loaf of bread, and it multiplied to feed five thousand people. If you want your substance to multiply and increase, then bless it. Here are seven things within your household that you can bless.

• *Bless all of the things you own*

Obed-Edom and his family took care of the Ark of God for three months, and God rewarded them for their act of stewardship: "And the LORD blessed the house of Obed-Edom and all that he had" (1 Chronicles 13:14).

When Moses verbally blessed the tribe of Levi, he conferred a blessing upon their things as well: "Bless his substance, LORD, and accept the work of his hands" (Deuteronomy 33:11).

147

• Bless the works of your family's hands

When Satan approached God in order to gain permission to come against Job, here is what he said about God's blessing on Job's substance:

> Have You not made a hedge around him, around his household, and around all that he has on every side? You have blessed the work of his hands, and his possessions have increased in the land.

Job 1:10

• Bless your land and property

When Moses blessed the tribe of Joseph, he said:

> "Blessed of the LORD is his land, with the precious things of heaven, with the dew, and the deep lying beneath, with the precious fruits of the sun, with the precious produce of the months, with the best things of the ancient mountains."

Deuteronomy 33:13

In your family time of blessing you can bless your home and property with the precious things of heaven. We bless our home to be filled with peace, and we also bless it with God's provision and protection. (See also Ecclesiastes 10:17 and Ezekiel 34:25–27.) Before you purchase a home, make sure that it fits these criteria: protected, peaceful, accessible and affordable.

• Bless the womb

If you desire to have more children or to be with child for the first time, you can bless the womb the same way Elizabeth blessed Mary's womb: "Then she spoke out with a loud voice and said, 'Blessed are you among women, and blessed is the fruit of your womb!'" (Luke 1:42).

148

• *Bless the Sabbath*

Your family needs one day a week that is devoted to rest, relaxation and spiritual things. God verbally blessed the Sabbath in Genesis 2:3: "Then God blessed the seventh day and sanctified it, because in it He rested from all His work which God had created and made." Honoring the Sabbath day and keeping it holy is one of the Ten Commandments. I encourage you to honor the Lord's Day not only by resting and enjoying the corporate gathering of the body of believers, but also by verbally blessing it. David did so when he said things like: "This is the day the Lord has made; we will rejoice and be glad in it" (Psalm 118:24).

• *Bless your kitchen pantry*

In Deuteronomy 28:5, Moses blessed the kitchens of God's people with these words: "Blessed shall be your basket and your kneading bowl." The kitchen is always the center of family life, so bless it with provision, joyful conversation and healthy dietary habits.

• *Bless your future provision and increase*

Again, from the blessing that Moses spoke over the children of Israel in Deuteronomy, we read: "Blessed shall be the fruit of your body, the produce of your ground and the increase of your herds, the increase of your cattle and the offspring of your flocks" (Deuteronomy 28:4).

4. Write Special Blessings

At given points of our children's lives, we write special blessings over them and read them during our family gathering. The written blessing might be given after a graduation ceremony or some other milestone. Here is the blessing we designed for our eldest daughter, Rachel, when she graduated from high school:

"Rachel, your mother and I named you Rachel Sharon. *Rachel* means "beautiful" and *Sharon* means "fruitful." We named you after your great-aunt Rachel Sharon. You are our firstborn daughter, and from the day you came into our lives you have been a beautiful, fruitful expression of God's grace. Our family began with marriage and you were the first to join us. Our lives as mother and father began with you, Rachel. You were born just a few days after Christmas in 1985, and you became the best Christmas present we will ever receive.

"Rachel, you are our firstborn daughter and every day being your father and mother has been a delight and a privilege—we love you! Rachel, you are the strength of our right hands. You are determined and directed, ambitious and filled with passion for the right causes. You will never bow to social pressure of any kind. You will be a sterling leader of leaders. You will always know the score, but will never have to settle the score to get even if you endure a personal setback. You will always live above the storm and never stoop down to involve yourself with petty arguments or debates that accomplish nothing. You will always follow the cloud and never the crowd.

"Your creative gift of writing, punctuation and grammar will lead you into circles of prominence. You will develop an ability to define issues clearly on paper and sway your audiences to give you a hearing and many times accept your viewpoint. For you, Rachel, indeed the saying will come true: 'The pen is mightier than the sword.'

"Rachel, today we your parents bless you. We bless your future husband. He, too, will be a leader of leaders. He will be a humble man who will love, cherish and protect you as your parents have. We bless your children. May you have many and may they be just like you: beautiful and fruitful. Today we bless you, Rachel, to bow your knee all the days of your life to your Lord and Savior Jesus. He shall be the Lord of your destiny!"

5. Include Grandparents in Special Family Times

Remember that Jacob's life as a grandfather took on deep, rich meaning when he blessed his two grandsons. For many grandparents—who may have never understood the principle of blessing—this can be a moment of resolution and healing. This event requires more planning, and the grandparents should be briefed about what will take place during the time of blessing. I can promise you that a floodgate of healing will open when you bring grandparents into a family blessing time.

A couple in our congregation invited their parents to join them for a special family blessing dinner. The grandparents were briefed ahead of time and wrote out a beautiful blessing for their family. The grandfather had been verbally abused as a child and had never known how to bless his children. After he read the blessing, he was caught up in the moment and without really knowing what he was doing found himself laying his hands on his children and grandchildren and blessing them verbally. At the end of the evening he asked when he would be able to do this again. Triumph! Resolution! This grandpa's life will one day have a storybook ending.

A night with the grandparents is not only a time for them to bless their family, it is also a time for their family to bless them. I wrote a blessing over my wife's parents and set aside a Sunday morning service to teach about the importance of blessing grandparents. Here is the blessing I wrote for them:

151

"Father and Mother, Hebrews 7:7 says: 'Beyond all contradiction the lesser is blessed by the better.' Indeed, this has been true. You have blessed your children and grandchildren since infancy. Who can find virtuous parents? Your worth is above rubies. Many parents have done well but you excel them all. Your children now rise up and call you blessed and your own works shall praise you in the gates. Now the circle of life is complete. The responsibility of blessing is now in your children's hands. We accept that divine responsibility. We rise up and call you blessed!

"You, Father and Mother, are our treasure and joy. It is because of your steadfast faith, example of sowing and reaping and constant encouragement that we, your children, are serving God today. This day, dear parents, we pledge our time, our resources and the strength of our right hands to bless you. We bless you and say: Your future years will be your most fulfilled. You will be blessed with long life and excellent health, and you will see your great-grandchildren.

"You are now entering into a time of greatness as you soon become great-grandparents. Your world will never shrink but will always expand. You are not on the precipice of twilight; you are beginning to live in the sunlight as never before. All of your talent, experience and gray-haired wisdom is now culminating for this moment of ministry.

"Psalm 127:4 says: 'Like arrows in the hand of a warrior, so are the children of one's youth.' As you blessed us and launched us as arrows into our future, so now we bless you and launch you into your future. You will not go out of this life as a flickering flame or a dim candle, but you will be ablaze with the flame of purpose and destiny until God takes you to be with Him. We, your children, bless you today with happiness and longevity and we pledge to love and care for you all the days of your life. You will never have one day when you are alone. You will always be surrounded by your family. May all of your children and grandchildren and great-grandchildren join you in heaven. In this way we rise up and bless you and indeed you shall be blessed."

6. Share in the Lord's Table Together

Paul the apostle calls the cup of the Lord the "cup of blessing" (1 Corinthians 10:16). There is indeed a wonderful blessing that comes to a family when they share the bread and the cup together in communion with each other and the Lord. On the first Passover, God instructed the Israelites to eat the Passover meal as a family unit. The blood painted over the doorposts was for the protection of God's people, and the sacrificial lamb was the provision for their journey. There was to be one lamb for each household. The New Testament reveals to us that Jesus is our Passover lamb, so the Communion celebration should be celebrated not only corporately in our church services but also in our individual households.

When you receive family Communion I encourage you to read 1 Corinthians 11:23–32. Before partaking of the cup and the bread, let all persons in the family examine their hearts to see if they are holding any unforgiveness toward another person in the family. This can be a wonderful time of forgiveness and reconciliation. Share some of the principles that you learned in this book: how at the cross God crossed His hands and adopted each one of us into His family through the right hand of blessing. Share about how Christ became a curse for us that we might inherit all of the blessings of Abraham.

There are, of course, many different creative ideas that a family can develop in preparation for their own family night of blessing. Try and create ways of blessing one another that are unique to your family. If one thing does not work, do not be afraid to try something else. The important thing is that your night of blessing fits into a consistent pattern so that everyone in the family can adjust his or her schedule to be there.

In my own journey down the ancient path of the forgotten blessing, I have discovered that a family night of blessing is really a night of worship. A passage from Hebrews that we have already studied makes this clear: "By faith Jacob, when he was dying, blessed each of the sons of Joseph, and worshiped, leaning on the top of his staff" (Hebrews 11:21). A night of blessing and worship go hand in hand because we know that it is God who makes our faith-filled, spoken blessings over our family irrevocable.

In the last few chapters we have discussed the elements of the blessing, how to bless our enemies and how to bless our households. I hope that these principles will benefit you as you begin to incorporate the forgotten blessing into your life's purpose. You have been diligent to reach this point, and I am very proud of you! In chapter 10 we are going to look at one of the greatest promises in the Scripture: As we verbally bless others, God promises to bless us and heal our generational wounds.

~~≈ 10 ≈~~

In Blessing I Will Bless Thee

Unveiling Your Promises

"In blessing I will bless thee."

Genesis 22:17, KJV

Congratulations! We have uncovered an ancient pathway, hidden for generations. We have cleared away the thorns, briars and dead branches that accumulated because we did not recognize the value of words. We have seen clearly the effects of verbal cursing:

- Words can be destructive.
- Destructive words harm the emotional well-being of the next generation.
- Belittling words shatter a person's identity, making it difficult to maintain self-control.

- Iniquity will take root in that person's motivations and decisions.
- This iniquity will bear its destructive fruit in the coming generations.

Now let's review briefly what we have learned in our journey. In chapters 2 and 3 we talked about your *name*, and how God wants to change the negative things you believe about yourself. We discovered that God wants to birth a brand-new identity within you. In chapter 4 we discussed your *story*, and we saw that every life story has four elements: a setting, a conflict, a climax and a resolution. We saw that unless a person finds healing for the conflicts endured in his childhood setting, his life story will never reach the climactic moment of victory over the past. Instead he, in turn, will inflict the tragedy of his story on the coming generation. We also saw in chapter 4 that it is imperative for a person who has been uncovered by verbal abuse to surrender his self-protective self-sufficiency.

In chapter 5 we discussed your *journey*. We found that oftentimes we look at our lives as a series of dots that don't connect. In actuality, every aspect and moment of your life journey is a part of God's handiwork, and in the end there will be a beautifully stitched quilt representing your life.

In chapter 6 we looked at your *value* in God's eyes, and discovered that God has placed His right hand of blessing upon your head. In chapters 7, 8 and 9 we discovered your *purpose* as we learned the elements of blessing, how to bless our enemies and how to bless our households.

In this final chapter we are going to unveil your *promise*, and we will see that in our blessing of others, God promises to bless us.

I said something in chapter 1 that I want to repeat here because it is so important: *I am convinced that through-*

out redemptive history God has ordained that the verbal
blessing be the key passageway that counters the effects of
the curse of sin caused by the Fall. A life of fruitfulness
awaits the person who uncovers this ancient pathway
and embraces the verbal blessing. Finding this ancient
path has been the endeavor of our study. We have been
seeking to fulfill the words of Jeremiah 6:16: "Thus says
the Lord: 'Stand in the ways and see, and ask for the old
paths, where the good way is, and walk in it; then you
will find rest for your souls.'"

This "old path" is filled with words—words of blessing.
This may be something of a novel concept for us because,
when you think about it, we live in a silent generation.
Between the rise of technology and the lack of modeling,
our words are few. Today when we think of enjoying a
"family night," it is generally centered on popcorn and
a movie; conversation is held to a minimum.

I have mentioned how most people relate to verbal
blessing only in the context of saying, "God bless you!"
when someone sneezes. This phrase actually originated
during the bubonic plague in the year 1347. More than 25
million Europeans died in five years. A slight sneeze was
the first sign that someone was infected with the plague.
No wonder your loved ones would say, "God bless you!"

Today we are dealing with a plague of generational
iniquity caused in part by destructive, bitter words, and
it is going to take more than "God bless you!" to heal
our generation and the ones to come. It is going to take
someone who will "stand in the ways and see, and ask
for the old paths, where the good way is, and walk in it."
It is going to take someone who will open up the wellspring of God-ordained, God-inspired and God-directed
words inside and begin to speak those words of blessing
to others. It is going to take someone who will believe
God's word to Abraham in Genesis 22:17 and begin to
live it out: "In blessing I will bless thee" (kjv).

157

The essence of what God was saying to Abraham in these words is: "Through your verbal blessing of others I will bless you." God verbally blesses whatever He establishes in the earth. This has been His pattern from the beginning. Look at Creation: God blessed His good works.

He blessed the sea creatures and birds when He created them. "And God blessed them, saying, 'Be fruitful and multiply, and fill the waters in the seas, and let birds multiply on the earth'" (Genesis 1:22). The next time you sit down for a dinner of poached salmon or curried duck, remember that the fowls of the air and the fish of the sea multiplied because God blessed them verbally. Every time I hear a bird singing I am reminded of God's verbal blessing over their future.

My favorite day of the week is the Sabbath day. It is a wonderful day of rest, enjoying God's presence and His people during the corporate gathering of the Body of Christ. It remains a special day because God blessed it verbally: "Then God blessed the seventh day and sanctified it, because in it He rested from all His work which God had created and made" (Genesis 2:3).

Ever wonder why five o'clock rush hour traffic seems to be getting worse? It is because God spoke a word of blessing over mankind when He created us, that we might "fill" the earth: "Then God blessed them, and God said to them, 'Be fruitful and multiply; fill the earth and subdue it'" (Genesis 1:28).

The words *bless*, *blessed* or *blessing* are mentioned almost five hundred times in the Scriptures. The two books of the Bible that use the word *bless* the most are Genesis and Psalms. In the opening book of the Bible, God was showing His children by example how to be people of spoken blessing. In fact, most of the concepts of blessing in our study come from Genesis, the book of beginnings. God led by example as He blessed the patriarchs and taught them how to bless their descendants. Midway through Genesis, we see God's people catching on to the concept of verbal blessing. When Rebekah was leaving her home to become Isaac's wife, her family spoke to her this way:

> And they blessed Rebekah and said to her: "Our sister, may you become the mother of thousands of ten thousands; and may your descendants possess the gates of those who hate them."
>
> Genesis 24:60

This family knew that God had ordained verbal blessing to be the fountainhead of fruitfulness that counters the curse of sin. Not only did they bless Rebekah to be a mother of tens of thousands, but they also blessed her descendants with protection and victory over the gates of hell!

And when Peter confessed with his mouth that Jesus was the Son of God, Jesus responded with a similar blessing of His own:

> Jesus answered and said to him, "Blessed are you, Simon Bar-Jonah, for flesh and blood has not revealed this to you, but My Father who is in heaven. And I also say to you that you are Peter, and on this rock I will build My church, and the gates of Hades shall not prevail against it."
>
> Matthew 16:17–18

This blessing was meant not only for Peter but also for everyone who would believe in the divinity of Jesus and confess Him as Lord. I am thankful that Jesus spoke this blessing over His Church and gave us victory over the gates of the enemy. Aren't you?

Still, we need to remember that blessings are conditional: They are based on our willingness to bless others. Remember that God said to Abraham, "In blessing I will bless thee." *As you bless I will bless you.* We find in Peter's epistle the exact same condition that God gave to Abraham:

> Finally, all of you be of one mind, having compassion for one another; love as brothers, be tenderhearted, be courteous; not returning evil for evil or reviling for reviling, but on the contrary blessing, knowing that you were called to this, that you may inherit a blessing. For "he who would love life and see good days, let him refrain his tongue from evil, and his lips from speaking deceit. Let him turn away from evil and do good; let him seek peace and pursue it."
>
> 1 Peter 3:8–11

Did you see it? Peter is saying, "Verbally bless others and you will inherit a blessing." The rich inheritance of my faith in Christ, my wholeness, completeness and the gift of divine health flow my way through verbal blessing!

When God called Abraham, He promised him something remarkable:

> Now the LORD had said to Abram: "Get out of your country, from your family and from your father's house, to a land that I will show you. I will make you a great nation; I will bless you and make your name great; and you shall be a blessing. I will bless those who bless you, and I will curse him who curses you; and in you all the families of the earth shall be blessed."
>
> Genesis 12:1–3

Let's take a few moments to consider what this means in today's terms.

The Power of Abraham's Blessing

If Abraham passed down the covenant blessings of God in part through verbal blessing, then we might surmise that every family on earth today has been blessed because of the Jewish people. Can this be proven? Think about this: More than six million Jews died in the Holocaust, radically diminishing the Jewish race. Yet, though Jews make up just one-fourth of 1 percent of the world's population, they have supplied *15 percent* of the Nobel Prize winners since 1899.

In his book *What the Church Owes the Jew*, Leslie Flynn writes:

> If an anti-Semite decided to boycott all the tests and cures discovered by the Jews, he would certainly open himself to a host of serious diseases. Besides refusing Jonas Salk's polio Vaccine, he would also decline the polio pill by Dr. Albert Sabin; the test to fight diphtheria invented by Bela Schick; the diet regime of Joseph Goldberger which has fought pellagra to a standstill; blood transfusion made possible by the work of Dr. E. J. Cohen of Harvard . . . the Wasserman test for syphilis; the vaccine for hepatitis discovered by Baruch Blumberg; streptomycin discovered by Dr. Selman Abraham Waxman as an antibiotic; . . . chlorohydrate for convulsions discovered by Dr. J. Von Liebig; and vitamins discovered by Casimir Funk. [14]

Let's also not forget that the foundation of Western law is the Ten Commandments. The young American colonies based their rule of law on the Old Testament, and the Declaration of Independence and Bill of Rights were drawn from the natural law of the Noahic covenant.

Whenever you turn on a light switch, you can thank Charles Steinmetz, a Jewish scientist who developed a concept called "the utilization of electricity." If you are in the armed services and deployed on a mission that requires a helicopter, you can thank the Jew Emile Berlinger. When you boot up your computer you can thank Norbert Wiener, a mathematician who developed cybernetics. If you are a physics student and you get stumped answering a problem, you can thank Albert Einstein. You can also thank Einstein for his help in developing the television. If your city is powered by nuclear energy, you can thank Lise Meitner, Enrico Fermi and J. Robert Oppenheimer. The next time you drive your car you can thank Siegfried Marcus, who developed the internal combustion engine. You can thank the Steinway Piano Company not only for their fine instruments, but also for being the first American automobile builder. You can thank Edwin Land for the camera and Benno Strauss for stainless steel.

Let's not forget to thank the Jews who contributed to the world of music: Irving Berlin, Oscar Hammerstein, George Gershwin, Artur Rubinstein, Herb Alpert, Burt Bacharach, Neil Diamond, Carly Simon, Simon and Garfunkel, Arlo Guthrie, Janis Ian, Carole King, Gary Lewis, Barry Manilow, Olivia Newton-John, Neil Sedaka and Bob Dylan. In comedy let's not forget Groucho, Chico and Harpo Marx.

If you wear a particular brand of blue jeans, remember that that is a Jewish name just above the right back pocket. Which name? Why Levi, of course—Levi Strauss developed Levi jeans.

But the greatest contribution that Jews made to bless all the families of the earth was the Messiah, Jesus, born of a Jewish virgin named Mary. God's Word was also written and preserved by Jews, and the evangelist who brought the Gospel to the Gentile world was a Jewish man named Paul.

One of America's founding fathers, John Adams, wrote in a letter to F. A. Van der Kemp,

I will insist that the Hebrews have done more to civilize men than any other nation. . . . If I were an atheist . . . I should believe that chance had ordered the Jews to preserve and to propagate to all mankind the doctrine of a supreme, intelligent, wise, almighty sovereign of the universe, which I believe to be the great essential principle of all morality, and consequently, of all civilization.[15]

Ever since Jacob gave the instruction that all of Israel would verbally bless others with the forgotten blessing, "May God make you like Ephraim and Manasseh," Jewish people have not ceased from blessing the coming generation with those powerful words. Their success as a people has hinged largely on their willingness to bless. They have believed God's promise to Abraham: "In blessing I will bless you."

From Generation to Generation

Three years ago, on a ship somewhere in the middle of the ocean, I was reading my Bible in the ship's library when a couple sitting nearby inquired about the nature of the book in my hands. People often let down their guard on the open sea; when you have nothing else to do, talking to total strangers does not seem that odd. I told them that I was reading from the book of Esther, and they smiled happily and said that they had read it many times.

I discovered that my newfound library friends were Israelis from Tel Aviv. Dr. Dov Shai, now retired, was one of six education superintendents who served over the country of Israel. His wife, Dr. Vera Shai, had just retired as the Minister of Public Health in Israel. Vera was a Holocaust survivor. She had spent several years in a work camp only to be loaded onto a train heading for Auschwitz. But the train broke down halfway to the

Nazi death camp and was towed back to the work camp. Soon after, the war ended and Vera and her surviving parents immigrated to Israel.

Dov is now writing his second book on the Holocaust. On my last trip to Israel I had breakfast with Dov and Vera in their home. I then spent the rest of the day getting a wonderful history lesson on how the Jews survived thousands of years of dispersion.

Beginning with the Assyrian invasion in 722 b.c. and the Babylonian invasion, which ended in 586 b.c., the Jewish people were conquered, removed from their homeland and relocated among the Gentile nations. Although some of the people returned from Babylon, as was prophesied, other conquering nations continued to invade and displace the people. When the Romans destroyed the Temple in Jerusalem in a.d. 70, the final, great dispersion took place; because of this ongoing Diaspora of Israel, Jewish people now live everywhere on the face of the earth.

In 1948, Israel again became a nation with borders—a landmark event for those holding on to the ancient biblical prophecies that the Jewish people will return to Israel.

But today there are still more Jews in the Diaspora than actually live in the country of Israel. Dov and Vera took me to the Diaspora Museum on the campus of the University of Tel Aviv. The museum chronicles the history and the culture of the Jews in all the nations of the earth where they have been scattered. The fact that they kept their faith, their culture and their families together in strange lands with strange values and morals is an absolute miracle!

Not only did the Jews survive, they thrived. How did they do it? How did they practice kosher laws and keep their religious heritage in the face of Western culture and ideology? The answer is that for thousands of years the Jews have practiced the principle of *L'dor V'dor*. It is and forever will be a major foundation stone of Jewish family life. Without the principle of *L'dor V'dor* a family would lose its faith in one generation.

Would you like to know what *L'dor V'dor* means? The two words are Hebrew, and they simply mean "from generation to generation." It is a biblical concept; you can find the two words joined together throughout Scripture. Other times you will see the word *generation* mentioned by itself, but it is in the context of teaching the next generation.

Here are a few examples from Scripture:

One generation shall praise Your works to another, and shall declare Your mighty acts.

Psalm 145:4

"My righteousness will be forever, and My salvation from generation to generation."

Isaiah 51:8

O God, You have taught me from my youth; and to this day I declare Your wondrous works. Now also when I am old and grayheaded, O God, do not forsake me, until I declare Your strength to this generation, Your power to everyone who is to come.

Psalm 71:17–18

For He established a testimony in Jacob, and appointed a law in Israel, which He commanded our fathers, that they should make them known to their children; that the generation to come might know them, the children who would be born, that they may arise and declare them to their children, that they may set their hope in God, and not forget the works of God, but keep His commandments.

Psalm 78:5–7

The principle of *L'dor V'dor* has helped keep the faith of the Jewish people secure even during the Diaspora.

In his book *Experiencing Spiritual Breakthroughs* (Multnomah, 1999), Dr. Bruce Wilkinson describes three kinds of generations. The first is the generation of commitment. These individuals have a firsthand revelation of the works and wonders of God. They have accepted the call of discipleship, and have genuine faith in Christ. The second is the generation of compromise. They are living in a secondhand revelation of God's works, and they are divided between serving Christ and serving their own interests. The third is the generation of conflict. The people in this generation are the grandchildren of those believers who had an encounter with Christ. The people in this generation are in conflict because they do not know what to believe. They have been mentored and raised by the generation of compromise, and they have never been discipled in the way of Christ. According to Wilkinson, a very small percentage of people in this third generation will put their faith in Christ.

For Christians who maintain the principle of verbal blessing, however, I believe that the outcome is quite different. Here is a scriptural example. Listen to Paul's words to Timothy: "I call to remembrance the genuine faith that is in you, which dwelt first in your grandmother Lois and your mother Eunice, and I am persuaded is in you also" (2 Timothy 1:5). Three generations of committed Christians! Indeed, Lois blessed her daughter Eunice, and Eunice blessed Timothy. Their faith was so genuine and real that Paul remembered it; it stood out. There must have been wonderful family times of worship and Bible study in that household and, from all accounts, the husbands of these two women had not yet come to faith.

Your New Beginning

Why have I taken the time to review here the benefits received the world over because of the children of Abraham? Why point out their commitment to pass on blessing from one generation to the next? Because you are of the seed of Abraham, and all of the blessings and promises that belonged to him are yours also. They are yours to receive from generations past—and yours to give to generations to come.

God cares about all of the families of the earth and He desires to bless them. You can swim in that stream of verbal blessing, or you can choose to let your tongue be filled with iniquity. You can shatter the coming generation, or you can bless it.

At this very moment God is crossing His hands and placing His right hand of blessing over your head. You make the choice: Will you bless or will you curse? Will you bless others with the forgotten blessing and open the door to God's blessing to your life? I am confident that you will!

So now begins your journey, dear one. Healing, wholeness and blessing will begin to flow to you as you begin to speak the words of this ancient blessing over your family and those whom God puts in your path.

But it does not stop there. You will also find wholeness as others speak blessings over you. Every blessing offered on your behalf is meaningful, but I think that you will find special benefit in using Hebrews 7:7 as a guide: "Now beyond all contradiction the lesser is blessed by the better." If you do not have a "greater" person in your life, you need to find one. It could be a biological or spiritual father or mother. It could be a pastor or Christian leader.

The point is that we all need spiritual covering. When the time is appropriate, share the principles of the for-

167

gotten blessing with that person who serves as your covering, and then ask him or her to lay hands upon your head and bless you. You may want to have examples of blessings for him to follow, or you may find that he is comfortable letting God direct his words. Don't worry if the person is not articulate or expressive. Remember that this is a new concept and it takes some time to grow accustomed to it. In any event, do not force things if the person is resistant to the concept at first. You may need to wait for another time or person.

If your biological father or mother agrees to bless you, be aware that something of eternal value will be happening in him or her as well in blessing you.

Now the blessing of a parent or mentor may not come every day, so how can you receive a spoken daily blessing? You can bless yourself! Do you remember our study of Tamar, a daughter of King David? After she was abused both verbally and physically by her half-brother Amnon, she tore her many-colored robe, as we have seen. But then she did something quite remarkable: "Tamar put ashes on her head, and tore her robe of many colors that was on her, and laid her hand on her head and went away crying bitterly" (2 Samuel 13:19).

When a person was mourning in biblical days, she would place her own hand upon her head and speak blessings over herself. Because the forgotten blessing was used so frequently, it is very possible that, in her grief, Tamar was blessing herself with the forgotten blessing: "May I be like Ephraim and Manasseh and forget the pain of my father's house and be fruitful in my future."

I encourage you to make the forgotten blessing a part of your daily prayer life. "Lord, make me like Ephraim and Manasseh!" I can tell you personally that blessing myself with these words has brought healing, wholeness and completeness flowing like a rushing river into my life.

The promise that God has given is true: In your blessing, He will bless you. Now begins your life of fruitfulness, healing and resolution. This is *your* promise—walk in it! The ancient path of the spoken blessing is before you. The thorns, thistles, branches and weeds have all been cleared. You have found a forgotten passageway to promise.

I pray that you will forget all of the toil and pain from your early setting and find healing from your generational wounds through the power of the forgotten blessing. I also pray that your future will be greater than your past and that your family will walk in blessing from generation to generation. Bless you! May you be like Ephraim and Manasseh—may you forget the pain of your past and may you be fruitful every day of your life.

Notes

1. Andrew Vachss, "You Carry the Cure in Your Own Heart," *Parade* (28 August 1994).

2. Alice Sare, *Defilement through Generational Curses Causing Arrested Development*, 4th ed. (Te Awamutu, New Zeland: Ezekiel Ministries, 1999), 4.

3. Bruce Perry, Duane Runyan, and Carrie Sturges, "Bonding and Attachment in Maltreated Children," *Child Trauma Academy Parent and Caregiver Education Series*, vol. 1 (Houston: Childhood Trauma Academy, 1998), 2.

4. Ibid.

5. Mitch Albom, *The Five People You Meet in Heaven* (New York: Hyperion Books, 2003), 40.

6. Ibid., 41–42.

7. Dr. Grace Ketterman, *Verbal Abuse* (Ann Arbor, Mich.: Servant Publications, 1992), 59.

8. Perry, 5.

9. G. Philip Ney, *Preventing Child Abuse* (Geneva, Switzerland: World Congress of Families II, World Family Policy Center, 1999).

10. D. Hemenway, S. Solnick, and J. Carter, "Child-rearing Violence," *Department of Health Policy and Management, Harvard School of Public Health* (18 December 1994).

11. Albom, 104.

12. Ketterman, 14.

13. George Barna, *Transforming Children Into Spiritual Champions* (Ventura, Calif.: Regal Books, 2003), 77–79.

14. Leslie B. Flynn, *What the Church Owes the Jew* (Carlsbad, Calif.: Magnus Press, 1998), 2.

15. Rabbi Joseph Telushkin, *Jewish Wisdom* (New York: William Morrow, 1994), 498.

Aaron Früh (pronounced *free*) is the pastor of Knollwood Church in Mobile, Alabama. He is a graduate of Bethany College in Santa Cruz, California, and Wheaton Graduate School in Wheaton, Illinois. His first book, entitled *The Decree of Esther*, was also published by Chosen Books. Aaron and his wife, Sharon, have four children: Rachel, Elizabeth, Hannah and Nathan.

If you would like to contact Aaron or schedule him for a "Forgotten Blessing" presentation, you may reach him at:

Knollwood Church
1501 Knollwood Dr.
Mobile, AL 36609
(251) 661–8383
afruh@bellsouth.net